invitation to WONDER

Praise for

INVITATION TO WONDER

"Elizabeth Ayres is Claude Monet with words, an Impressionist of language. Up close you are dazzled by the deft, perfect strokes of color and rhythm. Step back, and you see the picture in its living entirety, as words melt into light and shimmering air. The wonder, of course, lies in the melting: sounds, smells, heat, cold, hope and memory all conjured so instantly, so perfectly, it makes you feel alive, and *there*. This is armchair travel, the best antidote I know for too much city living."

—Paula Cohen, author of *Gramercy Park*, a Literary Guild/Book of the Month Club selection

"*Invitation to Wonder* transforms our ordinary perceptions into mystic beauty."

—Beatrice Bruteau, author of *The Easter Mysteries*

"Beautiful in its reverence for all that is nature, but nature re-defined by the author's own vision of it. We all struggle to find what we mean through what we see -- these words bring us closer to this struggle, this meaning."

—Richard Lewis, founder and director of the Touchstone Center for Children, author of *Shaking the Grass for Dew*

"This book has me remembering the rich pleasure of reading three essayists many years ago: Lewis Thomas, Loren Eisley, E.B. White."

—Rod Jellema, author of *Incarnality: The Collected Poems, 1970-2010*

"It's like peering into the heart of a flower. The earthy directness of the vision coupled with the depth of scientific knowledge makes it unique and memorable. Elizabeth Ayres can reveal the cosmos in a spider's web."

—Jan Booth, author of *Women Who Work*

"Elizabeth Ayres writes about the natural world as if she sees through a special lens that reveals to her what others overlook. Her gift to readers is an invitation to slow down, to see the profound in the commonplace. Her observations strike a chord. People respond, 'Yes, that's exactly what that's like, though I never thought of it that way.'"

—Rick Boyd, editor, *The Enterprise*

"Each of these lovely reflections does what a fine essay always does: turns a compelling lens on something we know well to reveal its mysteries and its startling beauty."

—Barbara Crafton, director of the Geranium Farm and author of *The Sewing Room*

"Most everybody in Chesapeake Country hears the poetry of wind and water, and many aspire to translate it into human language. Elizabeth Ayres succeeds. She startles us out of convention to think in new patterns."

—Sandra Olivetti Martin, *Bay Weekly* publisher and editor

"*Bay Betrothal* [is] one of the most poetic, beautiful love letters to the Chesapeake I have ever read."

—Ada Strausburg, the *Potomac Review*

"Born in Southern Maryland and living so long in New York, Elizabeth Ayres returns home almost as a tourist to discover and reclaim the beauty of nature's ebb and flow. The writing is gentle, yet it has a solid integrity. These reflections lead us to important questions that challenge our boundaries of personal responsibility without being confrontational."

—MICHAEL GLASER, FORMER POET LAUREATE OF MARYLAND

"The language in these reflections is at once arresting and liberating. The pleasurable music that emerges from each passage holds the reader in thrall. Elizabeth Ayres appears incapable of penning an uninteresting sentence, or a line that does not float off the tongue and sashay across the page."

—JEFFREY COLEMAN, AUTHOR OF *SPIRITS DISTILLED: POEMS*

"Like the vibrant landscapes she writes about, Elizabeth Ayres' language twists and dips, ripples and eddies, drawing us along as surely as the ocean currents. It's a pleasure to plunge into each chapter, to be refreshed by insights and images that nurture the soul and that, indeed, invite us to wonder."

—MARY REYNOLDS THOMPSON, FOUNDER AND DIRECTOR OF WRITE THE DAMN BOOK, AUTHOR OF *AWAKENING THE ECO-SOUL*

"Elizabeth Ayres sings of being 'mesmerized by greenness' and by daily discoveries of life's fecundity. These delightful reflections invite us to join her on the path of learning to love the world."

—JONATHAN MONTALDO, AUTHOR OF *BRIDGES TO CONTEMPLATIVE LIVING WITH THOMAS MERTON*

"Elizabeth Ayres' marvelous prose deftly teaches us to see, touch and feel the world around us through the wonder-filled mind of a child, for whom everything is a shining new discovery."

—Karen Karper Fredette, author of *Where God Begins to Be*

"An invitation to reclaim a new, more intimate relationship to the natural world at a time it's most needed. Bravo!"

—Carolyn Toben, founder of the Center for Education, Imagination and the Natural World

Also by Elizabeth Ayres

Writing the Wave:
Inspired Rides for Aspiring Writers

Know the Way: Poems

The Ultimate Creative Writing Workshop
(audio album)

ELIZABETH AYRES

Veriditas Books
California, Maryland

Published by Veriditas Books
P. O. Box 968 • California, MD 20619
1-800-510-1049
VeriditasBooks.com • info@veriditasbooks.com

ISBN 978-0-9845178-4-8
Library of Congress Control Number: 2010934240

Cover Art by Maria Termini (mariatermini.com)

Excepting "Fossils," "The Bridge," "The Comfort of Green," "Raindrops in the River" and "Still Night, Twin Moons" and excepting the essays noted below, the work appearing herein was first published in *The Enterprise* newspaper as a monthly column entitled "Soundings," which began in August 2006 and continues to this date.

The following first appeared in *Bay Weekly*, the independent paper of Maryland's Annapolis capital region, in print and online (www.bayweekly.com). That publication's titles, when different from the author's, are indicated in parenthesis: "Bay Betrothal" ("The Pleasures of Summer"); "Passing By" ("The Passing of Maryland's Tobacco Calendar"); "Catching the Light;" "The Zone" ("The Swash Zone");" "The Work We Do" ("The Work We Do Is Ground Away"); "Thanksgiving Hallelujah" ("Preparing for Thanksgiving"); "The Journey" ("In One Sun's Setting Another Rises"); "Equinox" (Gallivanting on a Good Friday Full Moon"); "Blue Crab Etude;" "Remembering the Future" ("On Memorial Day"); "Sea Nettles;" "Berries, Blossoms, Bunting" ("Declarations of Independence"); "Vigil" ("Celestial Navigation"); "Notes of a Native Daughter" ("Filling the Crater in Our Hearts").

to
my Chesapeake Bay homeland

"You called to me,
you shattered my deafness,
you put my blindness to flight."
—Augustine of Hippo, *Confessions*

TABLE OF CONTENTS

Acknowledgements....................................i
Introduction..v

SPRING

Prequel to 'Spring' 3
Song Flows Forth 6
Passing By 10
Equinox 14
Ghost Ship 18
Point of Intersection 21
Praising Green 24
Reconciling with April 27
What the Light Calls Forth 30
Maytime Musings 33
The Bridge 37
Remembering the Future 41
Seedsong: An Elegy 45

SUMMER

Prequel to 'Summer' 51
Bay Betrothal 54
The Comfort of Green 58
Barnacles and Tides 62
The Gift 66
The Pier 69
The Zone 73
Sea Nettles 77
Woodswalk 81
Blue Crab Etude 84
Butterfly Q & A 88
Berries, Blossoms, Bunting 92
The Gathering 96
Mimosa Moment 99

AUTUMN

Prequel to 'Autumn' 105
The Work We Do 108
Knowing the Way by Water 112
Bones 116
A Slow and Gentle Easing 120
Raindrops in the River 123
Fossils 126
Vigil 133
Baking for the Holidays 137
Joe's Garden 140
Thanksgiving Reverie 143
Thanksgiving Hallelujah 147
The Moon of My Belonging 151
The Barn 154
In Praise of Surf 158

WINTER

Prequel to 'Winter' 163
The Field 166
Catching the Light 170
The Fulcrum 174
Blue Moon 177
The Journey 180
Notes of a Native Daughter 184
Shadows 189
Everything Curves 193
Clouds 197
Cardinals 201
We Shall Be Changed 204
Keeper of the Light 207
A Different Kind of Wonderful 210
Rock Chorus 213
Still Night, Twin Moons 216
Deciphering the Season 221

Afterword by Tom Horton 225

ACKNOWLEDGEMENTS

Our English word 'gratitude' comes from the Latin word for 'gift.' The recognition that these reflections deserved to be published was a huge gift bestowed by Sandra Olivetti Martin, publisher and editor of *Bay Weekly,* the independent paper of Maryland's Annapolis capital region, in print and online (www.bayweekly.com). She was the first to publish that which was first written.

And by Susan Craton, community editor of the newspaper *The Enterprise*. She went out on a limb to make space for the *Soundings* column, and Rick Boyd, editor of that paper, also supported the experiment.

And by Barbara Crafton, who has been sharing these essays with visitors to her online institute of everyday spirituality, the Geranium Farm (www.geraniumfarm.org) for several years.

And by Sr. Catherine Grace, CHS, who carried the reflections on her *Grace-full Thoughts* blog (www.srcgchs.wordpress.com), then created and maintained the *Invitation to Wonder* blog (www.elizabethayres.wordpress.com) to give them a larger readership.

Friendship is a gift. Through all the ups and downs, ins and outs, steps back and steps forward involved in writing and publishing a book, these friends were present, offering encouragement and, often, hankies: Jane Sypher, Candy Cummings, Rhoda Neshama Waller, Karen Karper Fredette, Ton Jan Booth, Ton Haak, Mark Huthmacher, Liz Ward, Carolyn Egeli, Kellie Gofus, Mary Reynolds Thompson. (Extra gold stars to Ton, Jan and Mary, who provided invaluable editorial assistance.)

Companionship is a gift. My two cats, Sumi and Cricket, have been offering that for 12 and 9 years, respectively.

Love is the best gift of all. Jeff Ault has made a most significant contribution in that regard.

And to anyone who read one of these reflections and said, "I loved it!" or "That was wonderful!" I give a hearty, "Thanks!"

INTRODUCTION

"The world will never starve for want of wonders, but only from want of wonder."

—G. K. CHESTERTON

When I was in college, our class read "Ode on a Grecian Urn" by John Keats. I clearly remember scoffing at those famous last two lines: "'Beauty is truth, truth beauty,' – that is all/Ye know on earth, and all ye need to know." How stupid, I thought. How can people say this guy's a great poet, when he's foisting nonsense off on us like something we can rely on?

I was young, and angry. I wanted life to make sense – it didn't. I wanted certainty – none could be found. Keats' words disappointed me, epitomizing all the broken promises and frustrated hopes the world had so far proffered, so I marched off to find a more substantial truth.

Flash forward to now. I'm walking somewhere, and I'm startled by the vivid purple tips of a seed-blown thistle flower. Or maybe I'm driving, and the shape of a drifting cloud catches me off-guard. Or I'm sitting in my back yard, and some bird pipes up with a burst of song, and for one instant I'm freed from my tiny self's illusory baggage of broken promises and frustrated hopes, catapulted to a place that's large and real and true. I need to name it, the place where I've been, so I smile and think, "O, that's beautiful."

The dictionary defines 'wonder' as "the emotion excited by the perception of something novel, unexpected or inexplicable; astonishment mingled with perplexity or bewildered curiosity." Just last night, on my way to an appointment, I got shanghaied by a bunch of trees. The road was lined with them, an effervescence of mimosa, their flowers like fans, ballerinas, balloons, butterflies, I couldn't help myself, I had to get up close. I parked my car by the side of the road, scrambled over a ditch, up a hill, into a whorl of scent as delicate as pink cobwebs, as fragile as blushing soap bubbles. I thought, "How is it I

have lived so long burdened by gravity when all along a nirvana of weightlessness has been waiting for me, disguised as a simple perfume?"

I plucked one gossamer blossom. Tickled my cheek into a fuzzy giggle with it. Painted the flesh of one arm incandescent with the brush of it. I noticed the buds. Tight green knobs. Impenetrable verdigris knots. Solid, infrangible nodes from which nothing could emerge and yet, from each hard pebble an effusion of soft threads had burst. A silky, extravagant testament to the unexpected. As surprising a witness to inexplicable potential as pink cobwebs of morning spun from the black silk of night. Surely they would understand, the people expecting me? Surely they would understand if I called and said, "I'm sorry, I can't come now, my emotions are all excited by the perception of something novel, but please, do go on without me."

Well, maybe not. Do you remember the Christmas hymn that begins, "I wonder as I wander...?" That's what I've been doing these past few years, carrying my notebook around the seasons the way a landscape painter might lug an easel, and the reflections you're about to read are the result of all my gazing, gaping and gawking. I've been mesmerized by the flick, flash, fizz of a cardinal with its dash, startle, zing of red on a snow-clad branch. I've been entranced by an old stump with its worn, pleated bark. I've been beguiled by April raindrops, tat, tat, tat on the grass, like tiny claws. Intoxicated by a summer breeze, aslant with wings and tangled with warbles, trills and whistles. Spellbound by dawn, when an incoming tide of light submerges, one by one, the sky's small pebbles of light. Awed by sunset, when clouds turn into carnelian cobblestones and colored leaves turn to jewels.

I've been bewildered by the very nature of light, which Einstein himself called a mystery: pure energy interfacing with matter at its electrical and magnetic levels. How fascinating: a bird's song is different than its call, and birds rehearse their songs in dreams. How clever: we invented leap year as an anchor cast out to stop calendar dates from drifting. How profound: green means carbon dioxide for oxygen, light for food. Green is our very breath, the primal exchange from which our planet evolved.

And I've been taught. In a skeletal wood, in winter, amidst the serpentine twists and rope-like curves of tree limbs, I learned that the fundamental architecture of any life is beautiful – despite or yes, because of, its fits and starts, strides and missteps. Ambling along the beach in summer, in that dizzying zone where the tide's uprush and backwash meet, I discovered humanity itself, traipsing along a giddy brink, its backwash of past desires colliding with its uprush of future needs. And once, I thought I saw God, but it was only autumn sunlight trembling onto leaves as they fluttered in the wind. It was just the wobble and jog, shudder and shake of leafshadows, a spotted dotted leafsong, a stippled spangled leaf-dance, a freckled flash of leaf-fingers playing the keyboard that was me, releasing from my heart a splash of leafnotes, presto-change-o, abraka-zam, I became music, I became dance, my face sported a leafsmile, my soul clapped leafhands in wonder and delight.

I grew up in Southern Maryland, on Mill Creek, which flows into the Chesapeake Bay, which spills into the Atlantic Ocean. I spent most of my life in exile, I know that now, banished by forces and factors to New York City, where, in the ebb and flow of traffic and ambition, I could hardly find the moon amidst the street lights. After 27 years in Manhattan, I moved to the high desert of northern New Mexico, where the moon was sterling silver in an onyx sky. She gave me a house of baked clay. Plunked me down in a barren, cratered landscape uncannily like her own: flecked with silver mica, pocked with ancient rocks. Even at her first quarter, the very ground swelled with light. By the full, I who had once dismissed the moon learned my own insignificance.

Now I have returned to St. Mary's County, Maryland, a peninsula which juts into the Chesapeake Bay across three rivers, like a long narrow pier. The sky is a blue-black mussel shell; the moon, its mother-of-pearl glow. She rises over rippled, wavering waters to see herself reflected in a thousand silver chips. She listens to a thousand conversations between soft night breezes and sea grass, murmuring insects and creaking pines, dry leaves and prowling critters, waves and the foam-gilt shore. This is her family. She is at home here. And if the moon be any judge, so am I.

Which brings me back to Keats. "Truth is beauty, beauty truth." Based on my own experience with nature, I would phrase it a little differently. I would say: the beauty in which we dwell is the truth that dwells within us. And I would even be so bold as to make this claim: the musings you're about to read begin in Southern Maryland but end in the territory we all share, which I think  of as the land of our belonging. Where earth and sea and sky melt away, having transported us – *via* wonder and awe and mystery – to a moment of inexplicable potential, where the weighty worries of the world fall away and we are free – free! – to discover what really matters.

For many years, I taught in a project called Poets-in-the-Schools. On the first day of my residency, I'd get the children all fired up about writing. To prepare for my next session, I'd always ask the teachers to give their kids time to make a folder in which they could keep the poems they'd be creating during my visits. I've seen hundreds of these charming artifacts, but I *remember* one. A boy made it. Out of purple construction paper. Decorated it with pirate flags, skulls and crossed bones, swords dripping with blood, airplanes, rocket ships and racing cars. Then scrawled across the front, in huge block letters: POETRY IS MY WAY TO LIVE. That child saw what the great poet William Carlos Williams saw when he wrote – I paraphrase – "There is no news in poetry, yet people die in anguish every day for lack of what is found there."

There is no news in, say, a weed-sotted, sapling-sown, straw-stubbled field, where wild birds and bent flowers thrive. Yet, when I drive by on the crowded highway, I notice how the field yawns in the midst of concrete and brick: flutter of peace, sigh of silence, one breath, one blink, it's gone. The moment writes itself into my heart, and later in the day I recite it. Flutter, sigh, breath, blink. Amidst thoughts hard as concrete, worries dense as brick, behold: an empty field. Space for wild birds and bent flowers in a crowded mind, and I feel more alive.

There is no news in nature. Yet it satisfies our hunger for the good, the beautiful and the true. So no matter where you live, I invite you to wonder as you wander with me through the sea-

sons, in this land of our belonging, where earth and sea and sky meet and we are all at home.

SPRING

PREQUEL TO 'SPRING'

Yesterday. (You may start applauding now.) Yesterday, for the first time in some fifty years, I found a name for my first encounters with earth's fecund and seductive mysteries. I was three or four or five years old. Six or seven or eight, even, for this was a cyclic event, repeated every spring.

By late April, the exuberant yellow forsythia would have melted into green. ('For Cynthia,' my child-mind heard, envying that other little girl her bold and golden blossoms.) The pink and white bubbles of cherry, Bradford pear and dogwood would have burst, replaced by a thick, homogenous paste of green slathered onto every growing thing my myopic child-eyes could see.

I loved to crawl into the dense sprawl of bushes behind our garage. On that little hill I would perch, lost in a derelict jungle, sheltered within a forgotten tangle of stems and branches and leaves that would sport luxuriant clumps of tiny white flowers which I loved to eat.

I can still taste them. I would place one morsel between my front teeth. Nibble. It was bitter, and crumbled unpleasantly on my tongue, yet I sampled another, then another, consuming who knows how many ounces or pounds of flowers in this, my first and holiest communion. We moved before I thought to seek a name for my efflorescent meal, but yesterday (Are you still clapping?), along the fence outside the public pool where I swim, ah, the tangled green sprawl of them, the profuse white bunches of them. "Do you know what those bushes are called," I asked the manager, and when she said, "No," I marched right out the door, snapped off a large branch, tossed it in my car and drove to the nearest nursery, whereupon fifty years of unknowing melted with George's confident proclamation.

"*Rosea banksia*," he declared, "Bank's rose." Then he grabbed a magnifying glass so I could see for myself. Yes, each tiny blossom resembled a miniature rose, a whorl of white petals, and beneath, a swirl of green sepals. "See," George said, handing the branch back to me, "It even has thorns."

We get a big charge out of naming things. What about Adam and Eve in the Garden of Eden? What about expectant parents? Last week, I went birding with a *bona fide* Audubon Society guide. My forest was filled with mysterious warbles, tweets and chirps. His forest was filled with birds, the names of which he rattled off while imitating their flight patterns with his hands. I was impressed, but not at all sure I wanted to trade my experience for his, because once you name a thing, once you fix it, pin it down, it becomes easy to substitute the word for the reality. When knowing crowds out unknowing, there's little space for wonder and delight.

Shall we, then, put aside this season's standard designation to walk through its days nibbling every derelict moment?

SONG FLOWS FORTH

No alarm needed to wake up these days, no sir, not with what those birds are doing outside my window every morning now. I'm not complaining, mind, I'm just saying: one day, silence, the next, wowie-zowie, spring is here, ushered in by a cacophony, a commotion, an uproar, ruckus, riot of singing. Of warbles, pipes, whistles, trills, twitters, tweets, chitters, chirps, cheeps, peeps and that's just my house, goodness knows what they're up to at yours.

I got curious. All that hubbub seemed so purposeful. I did a little fact finding and now I know some things I didn't know before. All year, male and female birds make calls. These are short, simple sounds used for short, simple reasons: warning, flight, distress. A song is different. It's a complex, melodious vocalization with repeated sections. Males sing, and only in spring, because the notes they're piping forth are meant for one purpose only: to claim a breeding area as their own and attract females to it. "Here I am," that's what they're saying. "Above all others, it's matchless me you want."

The songs of different species vary greatly in complexity and number. The humble Brown Thrasher has a repertoire of 2,000 distinct tunes, while the more spectacular American Goldfinch has just the one. Individuals within the same species differ as well. Starlings and mockingbirds create unique melodies for themselves by plucking bits and pieces from other birds' songs to weave into their own. They'll also borrow sound bytes from cows, cars, helicopters and chainsaws. Because young birds learn songs from their fathers, certain variations build up over generations, creating a distinct regional dialect. If you've been supposing that bird songs are shaped purely by instinct, suppose again, because the aria wafting its way to you right now is probably more individual artistic creation than species-specific program. Experiments with zebra finches prove that birds actually rehearse their songs in sleep, using their dream time to hone a whole range of improvisations they'll implement come dawn.

Spring is a lot like dawn, don't you think? In winter, the earth slips into a collective sleep. Identity is lost to sameness: bare branches, barren stalks, short syllables communicating common messages. Come the vernal equinox, everything bursts forth into its own special glory: cherry tree, forsythia, daffodil, all are warbling a singular song that says, "Here I am, matchless me, unique, distinctive, one-of-a-kind me."

And every dawn is another spring, don't you think? At night we abandon the hard shells of our separate identities to sink into the fertile alembic of the unconscious. There we pluck bits and pieces from a day, from a lifetime, from the whole broad range of human history. Come the morrow, we improvise. Not for us the ego's generic, utilitarian call of fight or flight, no, for each of us only the true song will do. Unique, distinctive, one-of-a-kind me flowing forth into that cacophony, that commotion, that riotous uproar called life or living, or is it just called singing after all?

PASSING BY

No shelter here. No defense against the wind that soughs across the weed-wracked field to do time's evil work: pry the rotting boards off. Peel the rusted tin away. Strip the flesh from this old tobacco barn, pick it clean to the bone.

Like a come-hither finger, it beckoned. Parking my car by the side of the road, I obeyed the summons. Now I stand, shivering, as slatted sunlight casts shadows to replace once-solid planks, and derelict hinges dream of swinging doors, and a medley of criss-crossed beams yearn to bear the fecund weight of tobacco leaves curing in the dark, rich air. Except now the brambles creep in, and the moss, and whatever wild and profuse promptings cultivation holds at bay.

I remember how they were when I was a child, these early springtime fields. The white cloth spread like giant wings to protect the fragile seedlings huddled underneath. The plowed and patient earth, her furrows flung out like arms waiting to embrace June's adolescent transplants.

We weren't farmers, but in those days, tobacco was the staple crop of Southern Maryland, and month by month the growing of it strung taut warp threads of recurring sights on a year's loom. Almost shoulder height by late summer. September's workers in the rows, cutting the stalks, spearing them onto stakes, carting the skewered harvest into the barns to be hung on tiered poles to dry. December's secrets I learned from kids who missed school to stand for long hours inside those mysterious, gambrel-roofed hives, where they stripped and bulked and barreled the brown stuff. Then the beat-up trucks and horse-drawn Amish carts headed for Hughesville and the auction house.

We weren't farmers, but our everyday shuttlings – to store, school, church, doctor's office – flashed like many-hued weft threads through a fabric larger than any mere comings or goings. Harvests and earth and weather. A pristine, primal tapestry to remind us we are all just seeds in our season.

I wasn't here for the 2001 Buyout, when the state offered tobacco growers money to switch to other crops. Now I'm back, and like everyone else I see the barns won't survive the transition. Inside, they're filled with heavy rafters crosshatching a maze of small compartments. All that can be stored there is the hanging brown weed they were built to hold. Who can afford to maintain buildings that no longer serve a purpose? They rot where they stand.

This day, rusted bolts pepper the ground. Twisted shags of tin tumble from a fraying roof. White bones of vapor trails litter a sapphire sky. Cars roar by where silence once reigned, and some kid hunkers down in the abandoned field. His remote-controlled model airplane buzzes round and round in a noisy, futile circle. Buzzes round and round, treading the same worn out path.

Soon, the great religious feasts of spring will be upon us. Passover. Blood on wooden doorposts, the houses empty, their occupants fled in terrified hope to seek a future they name the Promised Land. Easter. Blood on a wooden cross, the empty tomb, its occupant come forth to tell us: we are all seeds in our season. This day *is* the Promised Land.

Last night I dreamt I was hoeing tobacco. I could hear them laughing, the men who built this barn. Who pounded in the shiny nails and thought their shiny thoughts for a new harvest. The auction house is closed now, but that's no never-mind, spring is here again, her come-hither finger raised, and yes, it's sad those old buildings are crumbling, but this I know from religion and the season: it isn't loss that defines us. Death is a question mark, not an exclamation. And while I can't say what question you might hear it ask, "Who stands at this day's door, knocking?" is the invitation I'll hear whispered every time I'm passing by some old tobacco barn.

EQUINOX*

It meandered, the path. It snaked through a tangled skein of bare trees and I followed. Twisting where it twisted close to the river. Winding where it wound close by a field. It made me giddy, that trail. Made me leave behind plain old mundane hiking to gallivant, gad about, knock around. Lighthearted, I forgot what was: a dull, cold day in early March, and remembered to keep watch for what could be.

The old stump with its worn, pleated bark. What if I were to pluck it up and play it like an accordion? The velvet, chartreuse moss. What if I were to fling it around my shoulders like a cape? Maybe I'm not even walking forward, I

* Author's note. This was published on Thursday, March 20, 2008; hence, the very specific numerical calculations.

thought, maybe I'm climbing upwards on a haphazard trellis of exposed roots. Or swimming. The rippled, wavy lines etched into the naked pith might be from some current or tide.

No surprise, when the downed dead tree spoke. With its ruffled frills of peeling bark stained green by lichen. With olive-striped butterfly wings of fungus fluttering along its length. The tree said, "Dying, I destroyed death, for see the life I've reinvented?"

Those words come back to me now, as I look to where the meandering path has brought us. Snaking through a tangled skein of days. Twisting. Winding. See? Already it is the vernal equinox, when light and dark are perfectly balanced. Tomorrow, the full moon, when waxing and waning briefly halt their ceaseless motion. Then Easter Sunday. Commemorating death's destruction and the reinvention of life.

It's making me downright giddy, this mighty confluence of forces, for see? It's leap year. Earth takes 365.25 days to go around the sun; so every four years we must disappear that stockpile of extra hours. February 29th is an anchor we cast out to stop calendar dates from drifting through the seasons. And see? Easter is always the first Sunday after the first full moon after March 21st, which moon occurs tomorrow: Friday, March 21st. This date is usually the first day of spring unless it's had to leap with the year, back to March 20th, which happens to be the day I'm writing. Easter has fallen on March 22nd only four times since the Gregorian calendar was adopted in 1582. It won't occur on March 22nd until 2285. Easter has come on March 23rd just 6 times, and after this coming Sunday, it will be 2160 before these two meet again.

It's enough to make us abandon the mundane, don't you think? 2008 is special, a gallivantin', gad about, knock around kind of year. I say we leap beyond what is – that horrid war, for instance – and keep watch for what could be. As they will Saturday night, during the Easter Vigil, extinguishing all light then rekindling the new fire. As earth does every year, all outward growing extinguished, then all the green rekindled. What if all the killing stopped? Wouldn't that be our downed dead reinventing themselves as peace?

Wouldn't that be like someone expiring because they've been nailed to a tree, then later saying, "Dying, I destroyed death, rising, I restored life."

All the moons have names, you know. Depending on the tradition you follow, you might call tomorrow Big Famine Moon, because game is scarce. Or Sap Moon, because the time for tapping maple trees is here. Or Crust Moon, because the snow thaws by day and freezes at night. Or Worm Moon, because earth worms are astir now, and robins.

Depending on your tradition, you might call tomorrow Good Friday. This, to my way of thinking, is a kind of anchor. An event cast out into the cosmos to stop our inexorable drift towards extinction. Whether you believe that or not, there is still cause for lighthearted rejoicing. See? The tundra swans are leaving for their Arctic breeding ground, and the osprey are returning. Winter and spring, dark and light, death and life – all these mighty forces balance out today. And tomorrow then tomorrow then tomorrow tip the scales.

GHOST SHIP

Someone told me she'd been sunk at a nearby marina, and now she's mysteriously appeared in Mill Cove, her once white hull stained and splotched, her anchor line slack, dispirited. She looks to me like a work boat, like she spent her whole life in hard service to some waterman, who spent his whole life plowing the bay's bittersweet furrows for its harvest of crabs and oysters.

As I sit on a log half listening to the susurration of high tide slipping and sliding into the reedy stalks of marsh grass, the hard edge of what was softens, blurring into what might have been. I see her flaunting a jaunty, white-plumed wake, dashing out into the Atlantic then down to the Bahamas. Her captain and crew toss aside their work clothes to don swim trunks and scuba gear. They splash into warm, sapphire depths where multi-hued fish help them explore coral reefs and shipwrecks. At night, the boat smiles blissfully, moored among fat yachts and sleek sail boats, her men off somewhere, laughing, slugging back exotic rum drinks, singing calypso, dancing the limbo.

Sure, and don't you agree? There is some deep hunger at the heart of all matter to be more than, to break free of, whatever constraints its form currently imposes. When we had that big snowfall in February, I found an old tree trunk stranded on the beach, its long-dead roots encased in ice which had melted, re-frozen, melted again, until crystalline stalactites pierced the sand, growing the tree into a new and watery life it never could have imagined until I came along and saw its inarticulate yearning, its groping to become more than, to break free of the constraints death had imposed on it, just as I have imagined this ghost ship into a whole new existence, and I'm wondering if this might be the gift we humans are meant to bestow on the Earth, on each other. Call it Easter, or Passover. Call it Resurrection, or Exodus. Call it imagination or vision or intuition. Call it whatever you will, each of us can do it.

Suppose, for example, you could look at your ornery, obnoxious cousin or brother or boss or neighbor until those hard edges softened and you could glimpse a yearning to be kind or reasonable or generous. Wouldn't that momentarily free someone from slavery to greed or anger or whatever? Or suppose you could look at the Earth until the boundaries separating individual objects blurred and you could no longer even say, there's a pine tree, there's a river, there's a fish, no, because you see the deep hunger at the heart of all these things to be one living, thriving, pulsing, begetting being, and if you could do that, wouldn't the Earth then smile blissfully, having sailed us away from the ghostly existence we are trapped in to the new and fuller life she has always imagined for us? Wouldn't we all be laughing and singing and dancing then?

POINT OF INTERSECTION

On any other day I could not do this: could not walk this beach past the tidal pool, its entrance a deep wide gash that obstructs the path of all but the most agile of jumpers or determined of waders. I am neither, especially when burdened with coat and boots, but today the wind-driven tide is so low it has stitched both sides of the watery wound together with sand, and I am free to continue on, carefully pressing my footprints – one, then another, then another – next to the tracks of a raccoon, until, alongside my unseen precursor, I arrive here, where I've never been, to sit on a log and savor this unaccustomed perspective on a familiar scene.

Other tracings on an otherwise unscathed shore. Scalloped ripples made by currents and waves. A herringbone pattern where wind and surf collided. A zigzag rivulet made by water trickling into Mill Creek around a mussel shell embedded in the sand. Everything seeks its proper route through life, and everything meets resistance. I trudged through deep snow to get to the beach today. Saw trees bent low and bushes flattened by a crystalline burden that shimmered, gem-like, in the sun. Heard wind churn through shuddering pines. So many, my own burdens, so frequent, the bitter gusts. Yet, the rainbow sparkle. Yet, the ineffable song.

Twice each year there comes a moment of pure and unutterable balance. The equinox. When Earth's axis tilts neither from nor towards the Sun, which is passing directly over the Equator. If, suspending their quarrel, day and night can equal each other in length, then perhaps there's hope for other forces of opposition. I affirm this daily, whenever I pause at the intersection on Route 235. A right, and Shady Mile Lane will take me back to the house where I grew up. A left, and Old

Rolling Road will take me to the house I live in now. It's the same stretch of pavement, though. An asphalt, seesaw reminder that there can be equilibrium between present and past.

Now we have this seasonal pause at the intersection of the year. Light and dark: different names for time's one road. What if, just briefly, we could call it neither gift nor curse, could shrink not from nor stretch out towards the event, the situation, the circumstance. What if, briefly, we could suspend ourselves above all judgment and allow the deeper truth to reveal itself in each moment of our life? Like those first astronauts who, hurtling beyond the familiar constraints of gravity and atmosphere, arrived someplace they had never been before. Paused. Looked back to Earth. Saw that the separations we believe exist vanish when viewed from a distance. Sitting here on this beach, I believe it must be possible. For me, for you, for all of us, with our quarrels, our many names for the one road. All forces of opposition can find a balance. The equinox tells us so.

PRAISING GREEN

Like a kid kept after school to repeat her lessons (I must not talk in class, I must not talk in class), spring's return has me filling in the blank lines of every day's page with endless variations on one simple theme: green, green, green, green, green, green, green. Everywhere I go, everywhere I look: green, green, green, green, green, green, green.

Green grass. Green trees. Green bushes. Green in long thin skewers, fat round dollops. Green edges serrated, green edges smooth, spiked green needles with no edges at all. Close up, green can prickle or feel soft to the touch. From a distance, green is an immensity in which I lose myself. An infusion in which I can steep. A silence into which I am gathered.

Green is strong and stalwart, reliable, but green keeps secrets, don't you think? There's some espionage going on between green and the season. To discover what it is, I turn to the book spring provides. Green. Chapter One. Chlorophyll needs every color in the spectrum except green, which it generously bequeaths to our human eyes. Chapter Two. Chlorophyll 'b' absorbs more red than chlorophyll 'a,' which makes it go ga-ga. Chapter Three. Concerned that chlorophyll 'a' might feel cheated, chlorophyll 'b' shares its energy. Chapter Four. Chlorophyll 'a' is happy and grateful. To show its appreciation, it gets to work making something chlorophyll 'b' can't make: sugar. Something we humans can't make, either: oxygen. Chapter Five. The chemical compound that stores sugar and releases oxygen in plants is similar to the chemical that forms DNA in people, who exhale the carbon dioxide plants inhale to keep making the sugar we eat and the oxygen we inhale.

Ah, I understand now, yes, that explains it. Why I want to call green my home. Why I want to fall into green as if into a dear friend's arms.

Why I want to croon green jazz all night long, until morning comes and I can see my sweet and precious green once more. We are soul mates, lovers, life partners.

Green inspires me, completes me, challenges me to be my best. Is there someone who doesn't have something I have a lot of? I'll share, like chlorophyll 'b.' Do I have some special gift? I'll use it to make the world a better place, like chlorophyll 'a.' I'll be everything my beloved green calls me to be: a perfection of give and take, an apotheosis of cooperation, and while I'm at it, I'll see what I can do about those fossil fuel emissions. People are putting out more carbon dioxide than green can take in, and we don't want to become the parasite in this wonderful symbiosis, do we? Because that would sort of be like two-timing a soul mate, not to mention giving the book a very sad end.

So I think I'll stay right here, praising green, green, green, green, green, green, green, until I'm blue in the face.

RECONCILING WITH APRIL

I asked April, "What do you think about yesterday's front page news?" She said, "Yes!" Then I queried, "When will the current war be over?" She replied, "Yes!" I pressed again. "What's going on with the economy?" She answered, bright and cheery, "Yes!"

April obviously has a one-track mind when it comes to the sociopolitical scene, so I got personal, raising an issue she couldn't possibly sidestep. "What about that?" I screamed, naming my deepest hurt, but she just smiled. "Yes!" So I called forth my second deepest hurt, then the next, then the next, a litany, an armada of wounds. I named all mine then started in on yours: abandonment, betrayal, sickness, addiction, I even made up some troubles no one's ever heard of before, but she just kept grinning, "Yes! Yes! Yes!" that's all she would say.

Exasperated, I turned my back on the month of April and went outside, slamming the door behind me so she would get the message. She'd be sorry. She'd feel guilty. And I'll never apologize first, I said to myself, hopping in my car, turning on the ignition, she'll have to beg and plead. I backed up, narrowly missing three foolish children playing hopscotch – hopscotch! – in the parking lot. They'd marked up the nice neat blacktop with a lot of bright, cheerful colors. That'll show them, I thought, driving over their board, although as I sped off I checked in the rear view mirror and sure enough, they'd defiantly regrouped to resume their silly game, as if what I'd done didn't matter. Plucky brats, resilient, just as irritating as April, I'll show them all.

I drove around, determined to remember all my grievances for when I got back to the house to have it out with April, but then I made a mistake: I rolled down my window. I heard the peepers, Earth herself crooning to comfort a fretful babe. I smelled spring onions, a warm, scented oil rubbed into dry, cracked skin. I noticed how the green was spreading like a thick, healing salve. How forsythia, daffodil, phlox, cherry, all had defiantly returned to play hopscotch – hop-scotch! – on the forsaken land. Plucky. Resilient. As if what winter had done didn't really matter.

"Yes," I muttered, grudgingly, as I passed a garden spangled with pansies. "Yes," I whispered, hesitantly, as I admired the lime-green fountain of a nearby willow. "Yes!" I exclaimed, downright exuberantly, when a shy dogwood peeped out from behind a sheltering pine. That's when I finally heard her. April. Begging me to pay attention, pleading with me to practice with her the one word that can make the difference between winter and spring, between grievance and possibility, between politics-as-usual and genuinely responsible leadership.

But don't take my word for it, test it out right now. Try "Yes!" like chalk on the blacktop of your despairing heart. Keep practicing until I come back, I have to run now, I have to find April and apologize.

WHAT THE LIGHT CALLS FORTH

The year is waxing, like the moon. From the dark and secret jug of night, the pointillist song of frogs spills forth. Urgent. Insistent. Pressing on the shell of darkness as if to crack it open, and every vernal pool and ditch now swells with the get of frogs: luminescent, gelatinous orbs a-quiver with new life.

The Welsh have a phrase, *pwdre ser*, 'rot of the stars.' Makers of legend and poetry claim that shooting stars leave behind a fetid, shining jelly whenever they strike the ground. The English call it 'star slough,' the French, *crachat de la lune*, or 'spit of the moon.' Scientists say it could be any number of minute organisms: slime molds, fungus, bacteria, all of which can produce shimmering, viscous clumps of color which excitable folk might stumble upon in pastures or forests where meteorites reportedly have crashed.

Scientists also say matter is slow-moving light. That is, matter sometimes acts like particles, existing at particular points in space, but sometimes acts like waves, cohering as vibrational patterns. My head can't wrap itself around these facts, but my heart whispers, "I knew it all along." We are all little moons, waxing and waning in response to the sun, which is present in every photon-bearing atom on the planet. Come tomorrow's Maytime dawn, the splash of birdsong will fill morning's bucket, the willow will pour greenly to earth, and every yellow or red or purple flower will spurt from its small green cup.

Come tomorrow, the light will unstopper night's dark and secret jug, releasing me from encumbering failures and torturous guilt, spilling me forth into the day along with birds and trees and flowers. The light will whisper, "It is I, it is I, it is I," and my heart will answer, "I knew it all along," for such is the destiny of all creation, to be one in the light.

I hear people talk about their vocation as if it were nothing more than their occupation, what they do to make a living. That's way far down the list of definitions, if you look the word up in the *Oxford English Dictionary*. There you'll see that the Latin *vocare* means to call or summon, and for generations people have understood a vocation to be a divine beckoning. Maybe this is why poets and mythmakers have been so eager to find evidence of extraterrestrial life in the shining jellies found in field or forest where some shooting star might have lain. We ourselves are star slough, spit of the moon. Carbon, nitrogen, oxygen, fashioned in the sun's explosive, gaseous womb, then released to press on the shell of darkness as if to crack it open. Every pool and ditch, every mountain and valley, every animal, mineral, vegetable swelling with the get of stars: carbon, nitrogen, oxygen in myriad arrangements of vibrating photons, a wholeness that the light calls forth, that beauty and truth proclaim, that omniscience asks us to know and omnipotence summons us to create.

MAYTIME MUSINGS

A knot is what it is, my heart, and when it needs untying, I walk in the woods, or ramble along the shore, or stride through some meadow under an open sky, it doesn't matter where, any door takes me to the place I need to be.

Home. Where someone will shower my bruised soul with soft whispers and sweet kisses: the sound of small wild things scraping in the underbrush, or the touch of a gentle breeze on my face, or the tender, glassine caress of waves on sand.

My mother. Who knows me better than I know myself, and speaks my true name when everyone else has forgotten, and answers life's triune interrogatories: who are you, what do you want, where are you going?

Who am I? I am this immensity, this tangled profusion of living, breathing, growing, changing. My name is sycamore, sassafras, sweetgum. If you call out to the wind-borne gull or hawk, I will answer.

What do I want? To be free. To dwell beyond the reach of mechanism and artifice, task and successful execution thereof, because beyond all formulation of petty desires there is the great, round wheel: spring, summer, autumn, winter, spring, summer, round and round, an ancient purpose, my only necessary commitment.

Where am I going? I do not know, and I do not want to know, but for this adventure I will need courage that rises like sap. And the exuberant, spontaneous wisdom possessed only by things that arrive at beauty through routes wild, uncultivated, unplanned.

A knot is what it is, my heart, and when it needs untying I go home to Mother. Who tells me what I need to hear: I can never be satisfied or content except with something greater than myself. When I feel worn and tossed about, like some little scrap of cloth, Mother's truth is a sharp needle, it flashes in and out, it stitches me back into the fabric of earth and sea and sky. When I'm frightened, Mother assures me all shall be well, and all manner of thing shall be well. For Mother's consoling presence I am thankful. Nor can my gratitude be measured by any instrument known in space or time. It is infinite. Like her. Through whom we all came to be.

Hallmark makes no cards for this, but Mother herself provides us with the perfect celebration: the month of May. Think of all those flocks, herds, hosts, packs, droves, drifts, swarms, covies. Skulks of foxes, clowders of cats, gams of whales, skeins of geese, charms of finches. All that progeny, issue, offspring, that hatching, spawning, whelping, those broods, gets, litters, clutches, farrows, sons, daughters.

Somewhere in all of that, you and I. Who are we? This immensity. What do we want? Alignment with this great purpose. Where are we going? We don't know, but for such an adventure, let's all ask Mother for courage. And the wisdom to journey by her preferred routes – those that are wild and unplanned.

THE BRIDGE

Long and thin and white, it curves across the lower Patuxent like a gull's wing. At its midpoint, it is 20 feet higher than the river is deep. At its midpoint, I am launched forth above broad waters into an open sky, free as flight itself. At its midpoint, travelers are suspended between two Maryland counties, and anyone who wants can listen to the bridge speak. *That which was divided is now made whole*, it says, in its native tongue of spinning wheels and axles, passengers and freight.

When I was growing up – on Mill Creek in St. Mary's County – Solomon's Island, in Calvert County, was a 10 minute jaunt by boat, or a 90 minute trek by land. Now I can make the drive in five minutes. Every trip across the 1.4 mile strip of concrete gives me the thrill of doing something that wasn't possible before, and I love to hop in my car and toodle on over to the Solomon's Island boardwalk. The bridge dominates the view from here. Busy and industrious, people hurtle northbound on Route 2/4, zoom southbound with efficiency, purpose. Doing what wasn't possible before. Easy access to the Navy base for Calvert County residents. Easy access to the Baltimore-Washington corridor for folks in St. Mary's County. Jobs. Tourism. Commerce. The bridge makes the Patuxent River the spine of a butterfly. Hitherto separate entities on either side of her shores can now rise up, flap their wings together, fly forth as one into a prosperous future.

But progress has its downside. The sound of rubber wheels slapping on asphalt intrudes on my boardwalk reverie, so I retreat back across the bridge to a favorite riverside park. Here, I can sit on a spit of sand, back nestled against the cliffside, embraced by gnarled roots, serenaded by insects and birds. Incoming waves break gently on logs slick with seaweed, peppered with barnacles. Sunbeams glance off the water's surface like Morse code. Those dots and dashes of light signal nothing to no one, or everything to anyone willing to decipher the message. If I were to wade in and stay there, my skin would wrinkle up like the rippled sand of the shallow breakwater, where tide and current conspire to leave a track of their wanderings.

Industry, yes. Beetles scuttle every whichway across the sand, purposeful in their chaotic scrambling. An osprey swoops down, glides away with a fish in its talons, and for just an instant, the curve of its one wing in the foreground merges perfectly with the arc of the bridge in the background. The crabbers are out, their work boats lined up like horses at the starting gate, the floats on their trot lines bobbing up and down like little ducks.

Last week, driving home from here, I rescued a turtle as it tried to cross the road. When I pulled over to get out of my car, the bridge in the distance seemed to give me a conspiratorial wink. It was just an ordinary eastern box turtle, helmet-shaped, splotched brown and yellow. I picked him up, he disappeared into his shell, but as I neared the grassy roadside, his head and legs poked out and he began a furious mid-air crawl. His eyes were fiercely intent on escape, and my heart melted with pity for the creature, so determined to fix his own destiny, so utterly helpless in my hands.

The Governor Thomas Johnson Bridge is white, like oyster shells bleaching in the sun. White, like periwinkles glistening on broad green blades of sea grass. It trumpets itself across the Patuxent River, majestic tribute to possibility, change, progress. Laudable purposes all, but not the real reason the bridge was built. No, this graceful sweep of steel and concrete exists so that, if ever there should be an accident at the Calvert Cliffs Nuclear Power Plant, people living below it in the southern tip of Calvert County will be able to escape southbound across this extension of Route 2/4, into St. Mary's County, hence to points north. Like that determined, helpless turtle?

REMEMBERING THE FUTURE

Like a bayonet brandished against the tide, the long, thin peninsula that is St. Mary's County, Maryland tapers to a sharp tip at Point Lookout, where the Potomac River meets the Chesapeake Bay. When I visited in early March, the day itself was at arms. A tearing wind that flattened beach grasses and twisted tree branches. Clouds heaped in the sky like heavy, gray boulders. An angry white surf clawing at the sand. Small wonder that the elements assail each other there, given the history of the place.

During the American Revolution, it was a lookout whence spies reported on the British fleet. Next there came the lighthouse. Next there came the resort, with a hotel, wharf and cottages. Pleasure seekers vanished when the Civil War erupted, so next there came the hospital, built to treat Union soldiers then expanded to incarcerate ever-increasing numbers of Confederates. Next there came the prisoner of war camp, but the prisoners needed guarding, so three forts were built, and in the midst of it all, a contraband camp evolved, refuge for African Americans escaping from southern captivity to northern liberty.

Such bald, bare facts. But what about the lives torn, flattened, twisted? Some 5,000 men, women and children died at Point Lookout. In Hammond Hospital, with its 16 spoke-like wings, its 1,400 beds a revolving wheel of pain for those laid low by bullets, bombs, shrapnel, disease. In Camp Hoffman, where, over the course of two short years, 52,000 Confederate soldiers were walled up, living in tents, with scant rations, in every extreme of weather, suffering from malaria, dysentery, smallpox. In the Contraband Camp, where hungry, frightened folk burrowed into dens in the damp earth "like beasts of the field," one appalled nurse reported.

And in the forts? That day in March, I roamed through the reconstructed barracks of

Fort Lincoln. Thin plank walls kept the wind out, but not the cold. In summer, it would have been an oven. I imagine I am a soldier of the 5th Regiment, stationed here as guard. I peer through the window, out over the earthen ramparts, to the Potomac flowing freely under an open sky. Home is somewhere out there, my wife, my children, my ease. Duty has brought me to this place of constant worry. Is that the wind roaring or cannon fire? Waves on sand or the enemy's boots? It's gall I eat with my daily bread, this perpetual fear of attack.

In 1867, Nella Sweet published a hymn, "Kneel Where Our Loves are Sleeping," dedicated "To the Ladies of the South who are Decorating the Graves of the Confederate Dead." This grassroots ritual morphed into Decoration Day, when flowers were placed on the graves of Union and Confederate soldiers, then morphed again into Memorial Day, which honors Americans who have died fighting in any war. Perhaps we'll call it something else in the future, if we ever wake up long enough to realize: all our loves lie sleeping somewhere, this whole planet should be festooned with flowers.

That blustery afternoon in late winter, I met Bob, a member of the group that's been restoring Point Lookout's historical sites. Two of Bob's ancestors were imprisoned in Camp Hoffman, and he served in Vietnam. We spoke of war, and duty, and I wandered off, down to the beach, where I found a clutch of feathers, the tattered remains of some unlucky bird's free flight. I thought, On my mother's side, my Georgia forbearers could be buried here; on my father's side, my German Jewish kin could be buried at Dachau; if I had had children, they might have died in Iraq. That's when it came to me, we are all prisoners of war, and according to the Geneva Convention, it's our duty to escape.

Now, Memorial Day. Would it not honor those who have died in our wars, to spend one moment contemplating peace? Peer through the window, over the ramparts? It's somewhere out there, and the taste of bread without the gall, if only we could fly free of this place where, just now, we all seem to be stationed.

SEEDSONG: AN ELEGY

FOR THOMAS BERRY, 1914-2009*

The day we said goodbye to you, a loon sang on a blue lake as clouds separated into white islands dotting a blue lake of sky. Shovels bristled in the mound of black earth heaped beside your open grave, and mountains leaned into each other like sorrowing friends. In the garden, seedlings bristled in their own black earth. Then a long line of friends filed past a fragrant stand of balsam pines into the meadow. Then it was done, and we all went home.

---

* Author's note. Thomas Berry was a priest, scholar, cultural historian, author and (a word he coined to combine geology with theology) geologian. His books include *The Dream of the Earth* and *The Universe Story* (with Brian Swimme). Berry taught us to see the universe as "a communion of subjects, not a collection of objects." His vision was deeply informed by a childhood experience in a meadow, described in another of his seminal books, *The Great Work*.

It takes time to hear the voice of a place. I think you might have said that, although they could be my words, or this woodsy fringe of the Chesapeake Bay swelling into thought – sometimes the connections blur the distinctions, and I can't tell the difference. This place speaks in the creaking wings of an unseen gull, its gray body blending into the gray mist as a dream blends into sleep. As Earth's dream winged its way into your sleep and, waking, you woke us all. There are no words on the boulder that is your headstone, but it's been calling to you since you were a child, that meadow, in its mother tongue of lilies and crickets, its alphabet of white clouds dotting a blue sky.

White mushrooms dot the wet green grass here. I stand on a sodden carpet of pine needles. A network of exposed roots meanders, like the ropey veins on an old man's hands. That one time I met you, we read to each other. From your work, from my work, from the work of a host of friends, all those words, thoughts, visions, dreams, all falling like droplets of rain, mingling, overflowing, seeping into the ground, absorbed, transformed, and look, Thomas, look! How the pine trees have flung their seed-laden cones with such reckless generosity.

Look, Thomas. In the sweet salt wind, storm clouds roil and boil, seethe and churn. White as lilies, black as crickets, every shade of gray in between. The bright light and the dim light, the shine and the shade, borne in each other's arms, waltzing across the sky. I do not know what happens after we die, but I do know there is some mysterious exchange between creation and annihilation, between possibility and the extinction thereof. I know this mystery is choreographed into the structure of galaxies and grains of wheat, and that we are all partners in the dance, and that the single yellow dandelion blooming near my foot will soon become a gossamer white globe. Then the gust of wind, and a thousand seeds flying on a thousand gossamer wings.

It takes time to hear the voice of a place. From north and south and east and west, a thousand gossamer stories, borne on the wind like seeds. Sun and moon, mountains and meadows, lilies and crickets and stars – you taught us to listen, Thomas, and to speak the truth of our own story in the vocabulary of our mother tongue. A language with no word for 'goodbye.'

SUMMER

PREQUEL TO 'SUMMER'

Where the Atlantic Ocean thrusts her salty fist into North America's eastern seaboard (Maryland, Virginia, Delaware, we call them) – that's the Chesapeake Bay. Where the Bay, in turn, wriggles two long salty fingers into Maryland – that's the Potomac and Patuxent Rivers. And where the Patuxent River tickles St. Mary's County with a salty pinkie – that's Mill Creek, where I grew up.

I learned to swim before I could walk, so it's no surprise that summer and water are inextricably linked for me. I remember my parents, standing chest high in the sun-sparkled creek while I dogpaddled back and forth between them. I remember my father diving down, my arms wrapped around his neck, then he would surface, laughing. "Wasn't that wonderful?" he would shout, and I would giggle my agreement. I remember mermaid tea parties underwater, and playing with the barnacles that encrusted our pier pilings, and the long, lonely half-hour wait after every meal, before I could get back to the element that felt so natural and welcoming.

The first time I saw the ocean, I plunged right in. I saw the other kids body-surfing – that seemed easy enough – but a slight miscalculation put me under, not on top of, a breaking wave. It dragged me under, churned me around, wouldn't let go until it flung me high up on the beach, gasping for breath, with scraped knees and a bathing suit filled with sand. The sea, I had learned, could be an alien, unfriendly realm.

There was a frog living in our swimming pool. The pool was old and crumbling – too expensive to fix. Clotted with dead leaves and stagnant rainwater, it became home to a rather stentorious and long-lived creature about which the neighbors teased my father. "That old bullfrog of yours, keeps me up half the night," they would mock-complain. But they didn't understand, and how could I explain, that every night he sang me down into his amphibian world, where water is our natural element and dreams a welcome form of awareness. Perhaps in this next set of reflections, you and I and that old bullfrog will sing ourselves into summer's magical realm.

BAY BETROTHAL

Ocean waves are horses with foaming mouths, ridden by witches wielding reins of seaweed. So say the Mapuche people of Chile, and who should know better? On a map, their land looks like a long thin blade of seagrass flung shoreward by the vast Pacific. Waves could be an angry Na-maka-o-kaha'i, Hawaiian goddess of the sea. Or a capricious Neptune, prodding at the surface with his trident to make a spot of trouble for some sailors.

Such stories came to me yesterday as I paced a shell-strewn beach, plucking at words, trying to describe to myself the look of sunlight on the Chesapeake Bay's wind-ruffled water. Gleam, glitter, sparkle? No, jewels are too inert.

Dance, laugh, play? That's better, more alive, but what about awe and reverence for something totally beyond, utterly other? Something I can never hope to possess or control, can only aspire to meet, greet, encounter. That's when I felt it, a primal need to populate those mysterious waves with beings divine or demonic, and like the surf so sibilant at my feet, half-remembered legends lapped the edges of my mind.

Later, I perched atop a wild spume of silvering driftwood. Amidst a flurry of scricks and clicks, a tern had coaxed its fledgling to a piling just off shore. She would skim the glistening ripples, swoop up, fall down straight as a plumb bob, disappear with a splash then reappear in an skyward zoom, fish secured in her beak. With a flurry of shrieks and screams, a young girl ran to, then from, to and from, to and from the water where it shimmied onto sand. Her father grabbed her, hoisted her up onto his back; then, the mother took a snapshot of the pair. A white-haired couple plodded along, their white-haired dog racing ahead in a flurry of barks and yips, chasing a lone, white gull.

Zest of Chesapeake, above, and below? From my sea-sculpted seat I pictured some of the bay's more exotic denizens. The exuberant bristles and paddle-shaped feet of the clam worm. The prickly bumps of starfish skeleton, poking out through the skin of radiant starfish arms. And, needing neither witch rider nor seaweed reins, our very own *hippocampus erectus*, the lined seahorse.

Could a more improbable creature be imagined? A horse's head, a kangaroo's pouch, a fish's fins, a lizard's eyes, a dinosaur's bony plates, a monkey's prehensile tail, a chameleon's wardrobe and wafting, skin-like appendages that imitate algae to fool predators. They have no teeth, no stomach, and scarf up four thousand brine shrimp a day. Seahorses mate for life, and only males get pregnant. Every morning of their wedded life, the blissful couple greets each other by linking tails, twirling around, changing colors, then dancing off in opposite directions.

A friend just gave me a magazine that is celebrating the beginning of summer by offering a guide to the pleasures of the season. I looked the word up in the dictionary. 'Pleasure' means 'the enjoyment of what is good,' and I thought, wow, those seahorses are onto something. How about getting up every morning and meeting the day with a zestful swirl, a colorful, impassioned twirl? We are, after all, improbable creatures, spirits wed to clay, divine sparks flung on the wood of this world in hopes of a fine, bright conflagration, or maybe it's a joyous dance our maker had in mind?

As I left the beach yesterday, a pair of swans alighted on the tidal pool. Partners for life, they say, although sometimes swans cheat, reneging on their commitment to each other. I said a little prayer to bolster my own commitment to fishing terns and shrieking children, old folks, dogs, gulls. Light playing tag with the sparkling water. Waves laughing themselves onto shore. All the sweet and yes, the sour this day, this life shall offer. We are very, very good together.

◎ ◎ ◎

THE COMFORT OF GREEN

If you could just suspend your disbelief for a moment. Dismiss your need for empirical evidence. Imagine with me that, behind its closed and virgin eyelids, the unborn child sees green. Green the jungle waters of the amniotic sac, the enfolding darkness, the warm, protected tides. Green the silence, all passion and strife muffled, far away. Green the growing in that nine-month cushioned ride.

Do I exaggerate? Maybe, but scientifically speaking, green is life. Consider those two Greek words, *chloros*, green and *phyllon*, leaf. Chlorophyll is the molecule that uses the energy of sunlight to make carbohydrates from CO_2 and water. It absorbs well in the blue and red but poorly in the green portions of the spectrum, which is why tissue containing the molecule appears green. Green is our very breath, the primal exchange from which our planet evolved: carbon dioxide for oxygen, light for food.

I am mesmerized by green, now that I'm living in Chesapeake Country after a lifetime away. Thirty years in the concrete wilderness of Manhattan. Five on the vast gray mesas of northern New Mexico. Forgive my hyperbole, but as I drive down the street I am convinced that the woods are unable to contain their joy at my arrival. See how they run right down to the edge of the pavement, to gather me into their arms?

Back in New Mexico, people prided themselves on their love for the austere beauty of the high desert. "I had to go east to see my mother," someone might say. "There was all that *broccoli.*" And everyone would laugh knowingly. As if disdain could compensate for what we lacked: the consoling, companioning presence of things green and growing.

I walk down any road, enchanted. Green is a riotous abundance, an effervescence spilling forth, a verdant champagne. I see birds on lawns, telephone poles, I hear them chirp or twitter. But when they disappear into the exuberant mass of trees, they become something else: the green beak of the living world, piping its very own song.

Green beckons, like a crooked finger. Seduces, like a whispered secret. I sit on my friend's deck, staring intently into the woods that surround her house. Inside that luxurious flourishing I detect a pale emerald glow. Magic? Yes, but thoroughly explicable. Plant pigments accept all other colors but reject green, which then builds up a kind of spectral surplus that transfuses what light remains. Botanists call it "the green window." I prefer to think that the sun threads her darting needles with green to stitch us all together. Trees, bushes, birds, people ... we are all one fabric, one whole and arboreal cloth. What to do when the scissors go snip, snip, snip?

When I found my new house, I rejoiced, for behind me lay a thick expanse of trees. I moved in on a Monday, set up my back bedroom office to green applause. On Friday, I swear, just four days later, I stumbled sleepily into my office to see what all the noise was about. Outside I saw a vacant brown lot dotted with mammoth bonfires. Bulldozers roved among the burning piles like grazing dinosaurs. The herbaceous monsters had devoured my woods, quite literally, overnight. There's a road back there now, an inert ribbon of cement, and soon more people will come, I have counted hookups for at least a dozen houses. The people will eat and drink, work and play, but where will be the comfort of green? Farther and farther away, I suppose. And if the story of my homecoming repeats itself – as it will – I fear we are very busy sending ourselves into exile.

No conclusions here. From the green heart of the growing world a green pulse continues to throb. I know what it's like, to be cut loose from that umbilical cord, so I just hope we can all stay connected to it for as long as we inhabit this womb called Earth.

◎ ◎ ◎

BARNACLES AND TIDES

Beyond the gasp of white sails rounding the bend, or white clouds drifting on a pale blue sky. Below the river's sparkling, corrugated surface, where dragonflies and seagulls chase the waves. Under the water, that's where you would find me most summer days in childhood. Sipping from my china cup at mermaid tea parties. Or watching barnacles.

Down there, everything was different. Land's crisp outlines gave way to a green-tinged, myopic blur. Floating with the current, my long hair twined around my arms like seaweed. The cantankerous buzz of boat motors mellowed. The percussive beat of waves on sand softened. And the thick white crust on our pier pilings blossomed into a garden of living flowers.

I could hold my breath well over a minute. Plenty of time to submerge next to a post and watch the pointy little beaks inside each hexagonal shell open. A delicate hand would emerge then. Spread feathery fingers. Wave them back and forth in a slow, languid arc. To and fro, a serene pendulum. From one side, tranquil, to the other side, hypnotic. If, breaking the spell, I would raise one of my own fingers and bring it up close, quicker than quick, all the tiny doors on all the tiny houses would close up tight. Then one by one, the mysterious inhabitants would come out again.

It was a magic show meant for me alone. A delightful game I could enjoy 60 seconds at a time. And when, last week, I sat down to write about tides, this memory washed up like driftwood. A little research revealed the connection, for barnacles are creatures of the tidal pool, that place where land and water meet for conversation two times each day. The waving fingers I remember are actually legs. They sweep plankton from the water into the creature's mouth which, along with its stomach and sex organs, is buried inside six fixed and four moveable plates.

Every barnacle is both male and female. One will send out a long tubular penis into another, which broods the fertilized eggs then releases over 10,000 larvae. These swim freely for many days, eventually finding their way to the upper zone of some new pool. Using cement glands, the larvae attach themselves to a smooth surface where water only comes in at high tide: pier post, boat, rock. On that spot they construct calcium carbonate houses with doors that can open to feed or close up tight to seal in water during long hours of drought.

The tide itself is a kind of door that swings on gravity's rusty hinge. Yanked open by sun and moon. Slammed shut by Earth herself. Vast energies swirl around us, and we can steep ourselves in those cosmic rhythms. The rising and falling of water. Earth's chest heaving up and down, her breath flowing in and out. The Chesapeake's length makes it unique among estuaries, for when one high tide reaches the head of the bay near Havre de Grace, the next high tide is just entering near the Bridge Tunnel.

It belongs to all of us, this music, no matter where we live. This bass and treble. These notes eternally shifting into new arrangements of high and low, wet and dry, salt and fresh. I think of other alternating rhythms: silence and speech. Action and rest. Love and fear. The light that brings us life is a tide, swelling and emptying from solstice to solstice. Hunger is a tide that peaks and ebbs, and we are creatures of many and various hungers. Forward and back. Near and far. Exposed and hidden. Reliable, the ocean's restless creeping, but other movements: not so predictable.

I'm not certain how much we can learn from the barnacle, a creature with no heart or brain. Still, there it is: equanimity in the face of constant change.

THE GIFT

The grass on the path is still wet with dew, still fondled by the pure and virgin morning, still shimmering in its pristine, inviolate genesis. I walk amidst a profusion of butterflies, ripening berries and fat white mushrooms, under trees that loom like legendary beasts. The thick air throbs with the desiccated hum of locusts, crickets, grasshoppers, cicadas, a pandemonium pulse that inflates to crescendo then deflates to silence for mysterious reasons known only to itself.

I push aside a thick, leafy curtain to emerge onto the naked apron of sand. Is that applause? Or is it harpsichord notes of light flashing on water's keyboard? I'm not sure, but I'm urged forward, to where the waves stack up in silken tiers on the shore, a tender and refulgent caress my skin yearns for, so I slip out of my sandals and into the river's spectral green realm.

Stiff, awkward grasses become pliant and graceful. Minnows dart around my feet, tickling my toes. Emboldened, I wade deeper. Every step sends out concentric sunbright circles from the stone of me dropped into this moment, this moment, this moment, until I stand motionless in the fragile breeze.

I imagine I am some long-legged bird, some shore-hugging creature unsuited to the open blue water where the albatross flies or the whales sing, no, I prefer my amphibian walk, neither of the land nor of the sea but of both. Like the great blue heron I am a solitary predator, hunting alone. Unlike the heron, I might not recognize nourishment when it appears, a thought that propels me to continue my aqueous amble parallel to the beach, looking for I know not what.

Could it be the feel of mud, so silky soft underfoot? The surprise when a startled crab scuttles away? Maybe it's the way the water swirls warm then cold then warm again that beckons me on. I can't name the object of my quest, yet, as I reach the narrow channel into a tidal pool I am excited, expectant. It might be just there, just around that curve, where the tide hurries inward, where floating leaves rush by on their secret and urgent mission, that I might come face to face with something hitherto submerged, hidden, undiscovered.

My friend's daughter will soon be married. Lela and Joel will push aside the thick curtain of childhood to emerge together onto life's naked stage, and I've found here the perfect wedding gift. I'll send them the wisdom of the great blue heron, a creature that is gregarious during nesting season, but solitary and territorial during the rest of the year. They'll remember to keep their marriage an amphibian journey, never losing themselves completely in each other or in their children but always holding onto the submerged and undiscovered mystery that propels us, for reasons known only to ourselves, to seek expectantly for we know not what. I'm delivering their present just now, in person, arriving to surprise them on my great blue wings.

THE PIER

These boards. Grayed from wind and water. Green-stained from moss and algae. White-streaked from bird droppings. Time-buffed to a rich patina. My bare feet want to linger here, flesh warmed by the sun-drenched wood, but memory scampers off to the sunshine of a distant day. When I watched my father build this pier plank by raw pine plank. Sweat glistened on his face. I sat on a freshly-split log stair, clutching a glass bottle of orange soda pop. Each of my endless questions received the same smothered response, for my father's mouth was filled with nails, but one question – What makes waves? – I can answer for myself today.

It walked with me through the trees, the wind, touching each leaf as we clambered down the hillside. I can go no further than this dock, but the wind continues on. Making for itself a moveable staircase of water and air molecules. Traveling across the creek, out into the river, through the bay, to the ocean. Clasping hands with other winds from far off lands. Dancing with giant currents that gyre and eddy around the globe in a planetary celebration of energy and motion that I don't have to budge one inch to join.

Through wooden slats I watch the water slide shoreward. Light splashes off its wavering surface and back onto the pier in a brightsome, undulating mosaic. Stirred by the soft salt breeze, tree limbs cast quivering shadows on cliff and creek, while above me, white clouds roil with gray as they drift across their own blue sea. Seagulls, ospreys, crows. Dragonflies, butterflies, wasps. The air is aslant with wings and tangled with sound: warbles, trills, whistles; the slap of fish falling back from their sunward leaps; and always, the liquid tattoo of waves on sand.

My trusty online encyclopedia tells me that, in physics, motion means a change in the position of a body with respect to time, as measured by a particular observer in a specific frame of reference. Memory records such changes, yes? I remember childhood, when the pier and I were not so weathered. The pier, too, remembers: its worn metal cleats still wait for boats that have long since been junked; frayed rope from abandoned crab traps still clings to its pilings.

And the beach remembers. This morning I saw 'coon tracks in the sand. The faint tracings of a meandering periwinkle. The short squat imprint of a twig that rested briefly then ran away with the wind. Every passing wave leaves its inky autograph: pebbles, bits of shell, leaf mold. The swash pushes sediment in at an angle; the backwash pulls it out perpendicular to the shore, hence, that zigzag footprint called beach drift. The pebbles remember themselves in larger incarnations: rocks, boulders, mountains. The shells remember their fleshy occupants. Since all life on Earth began in the sea, the sea itself – that particular observer, that specific frame of reference – surely the sea remembers us?

When I was a young girl this creek froze over every winter. All the kids in the neighborhood ice-skated around our pier. Laughter rang from hill to hill, shore to shore. Games of tag. Show-off stunts. The flash of moonlight on silver skate blades. Hot chocolate in my father's thermos. But the creek hasn't frozen over in years. Those giant currents are warming us into a future substantially different from the past, as just about any observer can measure.

Memory scampers off to the sunshine of a distant day. 65 million, 250 million, 488 million years ago. Planetary gyres and eddies, the great extinction events that changed evolutionary history. And now, something new in this cosmic celebration: the energy and motion of human awareness.

Over raised dots of sunlight, water's blind fingers play lightly. Flung against the sky, passing birds make an *I Ching* of lines long and short. The whole planet is groping. Stumbling as one towards something only we humans can imagine or create. We are not fallen leaves, floating helplessly to shore like shipwrecked boats, we can plot another course, arrive somewhere else, think up new names for a world no one has ever known before. Ours.

THE ZONE*

When I walk the beach – and I walk the beach every day, now that summer's here – when I tramp or traipse or amble or ramble along the shore. And the breaking waves are a white lace flounce edging the sand. And the breaking waves are a salty pulse coursing steady in the sand. Earth's heartbeat and my own wed together on the sand. In the splashing water I'm walking, looking down.

They call it the swash zone. Uprush meets backwash, inflow meets rundown, water's mantra of longing meets her sigh of satisfaction. Here is where dizzy collides with giddy, intoxication confronts delirium, I can lose myself in the

* Author's note. This was published on June 21, 2007; hence, the time and date references.

place that's neither in nor out but in and out at the same moment and hence, just beyond the reach of space and time.

Here is where you find them, on the pristine, virgin sand: old logs and wet shells being ground to slivers and glints. Flutes of driftwood, holes bored out by tiny creatures, and by time. Castles don't last long here, nor can footprints endure. And if you stop. If you halt your forward motion. If, standing straight as an arrow, you try to remain still as a rock, the sand will melt from under, mound up over, your feet. You'll sink deep, deeper, you'll begin to think you're rooted, that you belong here, but the tether is misleading and the mooring false. Your real home is constant motion. Now you must go on.

All a-swell the light has been, these past weeks. Every morning, an earlier dawn. Every evening, a later dusk. Every day, a waxing radiance, an almost unbearable fullness, like a woman in her ninth month. This year, at precisely 18:06 Greenwich Mean, the sun will be tethered straight as an arrow, still as a rock, directly above the outermost boundary of the tropics, the parallel of latitude which is 23.5 degrees north of the equator.

This day is our longest, this night our shortest. By tomorrow, our star's moorings will already have loosened. The sun will be one tick further south, our day one tock shorter. We're living in the swash zone now. The uprushing, inflowing, breaking wave of light has collided with light's backwash. Summer has just given birth.

Once upon a time, they lit bonfires on Midsummer's Eve. They danced and drank and sang, as if to match the sky's delirium with their own intoxication. Magic ruled, and midsummer night dreams. Children twined flowers around the horns of bulls. Young girls scryed for future husbands. Lovers leapt through flames then bedded in the bushes. Healers plucked their most potent herbs. The people prayed and partied for what the people wanted: health and wealth and fertile fields, fecund beasts, plenty of kids.

That was then. Now we're living in the swash zone. The backwash of our past desires has collided with the uprushing, inflowing, breaking wave of our future needs. Humanity tramps and traipses, ambles and rambles along a giddy edge, a dizzy brink. We cannot stop, we cannot halt our forward motion, we must move on down the pristine, virgin shore. Where every passing day casts up new questions. Grinds old answers down to slivers and glints.

Last week, as I left the beach, I passed a woman carrying her toddler back to the parking lot. "She's afraid of sand," the tired mother said to me, and I thought, Aren't we all? I mean, who doesn't want to run from a place where the selvage is unraveling?

Yet here it is, the summer solstice. And here we are, brothers and sisters birthed together in a newborn season, ready to pray and party for what we're ready to want, our outmoded longings washing out, our newer satisfactions swashing in, a hazy crazy maybe zone, a midsummer night's dream.

◎ ◎ ◎

SEA NETTLES

The summer solstice has come and gone, but the sea nettles are here to stay. I stand on the pier looking down into the bottle green depths of the Patuxent. The sun has burnished the air into a metallic amalgam of smells: wood, salt water, exposed barnacles, sea weed. Insects hum, a chorus that rises and falls, ebbs and flows like the waves. How wonderful it would be to dive off this hot pier into the cool water. How delightful, to leave behind the friction of every day living for a skin of liquid velvet. I could kick my way free of all worries. Back to the bliss of the womb, perhaps. Or even further. To some mindless, amphibian state.

Automatically, with the reflexes of a child raised on this river, I start to count the nettles.

There are only a few on the surface, but moment by moment more ghostly shapes arise from nether darkness into the light, like eerie, diaphanous negatives developing in a chemical bath. I give up counting: they are as numberless as the stars. Their umbrella shaped heads pump rhythmically with the current, and their long tentacles trail behind them in an entrancing, balletic display. That otherworldly grace belies the venomous reality of those delicate threads. Poison enough to paralyze a small fish. Deliver a sharp sting and red welts to human flesh. If I scooped one up in a crab net, it would collapse instantly into an inert mass of brainless, heartless, boneless jelly. Removed from the water which comprises 98 % of its being, the creature would dry up quickly, expiring into its trace elements of salt and protein with a faint stink.

I recall summer days long past, when this pier was a blur of children – cousins, neighbors, friends. A medley of legs and arms and laughter. Bare skin, wet bathing suits. A background drone of outboard motors near and far. While the adults were off somewhere doing whatever adults do, we swam, most of us, while some stood guard, furiously scooping up sea nettles in crab nets then running to dump them on shore. At regular intervals, pained cries: "I've been stung!" Or, "One got me!" Or just a wordless shriek and a churn of water as the victim rushed to shore for the placebo comfort of sand rubbed on burning skin. And after, a chance to exact revenge by taking up sentry duty, with upright net pole and vigilant eyes.

Yet we swam. I remember diving headlong off this very pier piling, eyes closed tightly, hoping to complete my underwater arc unscathed but braced for the awful instant of entanglement, when naked flesh would burst upon a jumble of slithering tentacles. I would fight my way to the surface then, pawing to rid face or neck of the adhesive, gelatinous fire.

We strapped on water skis despite the virtual certainty of getting stung while waiting for the boat to pick us up. When one of us would be put to bed with a thick paste of baking soda applied to a swollen body part, the rest of us went right on. Cavorted and splashed. Played mermaid or seahorse or water basketball, all in a gloriously adult-free zone, because grown ups were scairdy cats, afraid to take their pleasure for fear of a little pain. And I'm one of them. Too chicken to swim in this water now that the nettles are back. I understand they're particularly fond of the Chesapeake Bay, where the right mix of salt and fresh makes the water brackish, their preferred environment.

Life itself is pretty brackish. Pretty much a mix of salt and fresh. Pain of one sort or another is continually arising from the nether darkness. The dangers are as numberless as the stars. But the next time I'm tempted to hold back on living because of some possible hurt, I'm going to consult with the child I was. I think I already know what she's going to say.

WOODSWALK

Where I was is not where I am. That grassy, sunbright meadow. This dark shroud of trees. That smiling froth of birdsong. This somber silence. Purposeful, expansive strides brought me here. Now, my feet make hesitant progress on a narrow ribbon of path that curls and furls as it will, not as I plan.

I pause. My breath slows to match the dark and secret pulse of sap. I remember high school botany class. Water and inorganic nutrients, tugged from the soil through the roots and up along the inert xylem cells. The magic of photosynthesis. Presto-change-o, abrakazam, now the water carries sugar into the living phloem cells. Down, around, throughout. Yes. I remember.

How to breathe. Taking in air's rich elixir. Letting it steep in lung sac, bone marrow. Down core of heart, pith of soul, then through and out.

Pausing winds down to stopping. I sit on a moss-clad log, letting my body adjust to the stillness. Like when you walk into a dark room. The time it takes for your eyes to adapt is the measure of the brightness you left behind, and I've left behind a lot of churning. A lot of plans and schemes. A whole big enterprise that sometimes seems more an industry I have to support than a life I get to live.

As quiescent hush silences militant maelstrom, I am free to be here, only here, in the midst of this vertical embrace, this upright hug, this skyward clasp of trees thrusting up, up, up – I see them – of roots plunging down, down, down – I don't see them, but sense their blind groping into enigmatic depths. I can't see my own roots, either, but with the rising, falling flow of sapwater everywhere around, I imagine that the tiny hairs all along my arms and legs can become, presto-change-o, abrakazam, fine long tendrils growing me down into the earth. Finding me nourishment, and a strong anchor.

Still at last, I can at last take notice. High above, sunlight trembles onto every leaf fluttering in the wind. Here below, leafshadows wobble and jog, shudder and shake, a spotted dotted leafsong, a stippled spangled leafdance, a freckled flash of leaf-fingers playing the keyboard that is me, releasing from my heart a splash of leafnotes, presto-change-o, abrakazam, I am music, I am dance. My face now sports a leafsmile, and my soul claps leafhands in wonder and delight.

I rise, slowly, not wanting to break the spell. The path that had seemed so cantankerous and confused is now a loopy, meandering marvel. I guess it really is like Dante said. When he found his way to paradise. Because he let himself awaken "in a dark wood/Where the straight way was lost." I shudder to think how many paradises I have forfeited in my lifetime, and tomorrow, when I pick up the paper to read the news, I'll remember today's walk in a dark woods. I'll remember to remind myself, presto-change-o, abrakazam, we're all just waking up.

◎ ◎ ◎

BLUE CRAB ETUDE

Nana taught me how. No matter how early I got up or how fast I slipped on my summer uniform of shorts, top and flip-flops, she would already be down there in her sundress and hat. Kneeling on the rough wood planks of the dock. Chest butted up against a piling. Left hand working the string, right hand holding the net.

I see the scene so clearly. Those four, frontmost pier posts, darkly creosoted, each wrapped with pale twine. The cord plays out into the water at a wide angle to its tether on the piling, and no child of the river needs to be told what invisible tug o' war holds the line so taut. On the sandy creek bottom, a blue crab struggles to swim away with its carrion prize: a chicken neck tied tightly to the end of the string my grandmother painstakingly works.

On memory's split screen, I see a close-up of her left hand: the twine, threaded through Nana's fore and middle fingers, pinned in place with her thumb. Over and under. Thumb up, thumb down. Inch by upward bound inch, crab and bait rise. Where it slices into the water, the net pole appears to break, a distortion that makes distance hard to gauge. Speed is out of the question, the water offers too much resistance, so with a stiff right arm, Nana maneuvers the net's wooden shaft by quark-sized increments until the head is directly under the feeding, oblivious creature. Anything, even a flickering shadow, will startle her prey into its peculiar, sideways scuttle. She continues. Cautiously. To tease that awkward trio – crab, baited string and meshed hoop – to the surface. Then one deft, skyward jerk. "Got him," she says, grinning. I scamper off to the live-box with our catch.

Popi also taught me how, although kids were not welcome to join him. "You're too noisy," he would bark, "You scare the crabs away." So I would watch from a distance as he waded along the shore like some long-legged marsh bird. Pant legs rolled up above bony knees. Skinny calves protruding. His far off, silent prowling is keyed forever, in my mind, to the constant slap of water against pier pilings, against moored boats, against the endless beach where tall sea grass whispers *snick snick* in a hot, dry breeze.

Popi is a vigilant hunter. He marches all day from one end of our cove to the other, net pole cradled – shotgun style – against a bent left elbow. From that position he can brandish either end of his weapon. Wield the wooden handle to poke under logs and rocks. Or, like a bayonet, stab the hoop end into the water to nab his elusive prey: a blue crab, freshly molted, butter soft. Supremely confident in his ability, Popi refuses to carry with him any sissy storage basket. Instead, he returns to the pier with two or three huge jimmies stacked in the same net he used for their capture. Popi's grin is all for himself. Tucked into his chin. Elusive.

An etude is a musical composition designed to provide practice in a particular technical skill on a solo instrument. Pianists may turn to Chopin to learn their parallel thirds. Flutists might rely on Boehm for their fingering style. I could walk down to the pier right now and catch a crab the way my grandparents showed me. Or I could stay at this desk. Teasing thoughts to the surface word by upward-bound word.

And what of this perpetual tug 'o war called life, where a taut line is sometimes all we have of what we need. Where bait and prize are often indistinguishable. And there's too much resistance. Too long a solitary prowl. I know that ceaseless effort is the cost of all things hoped for, yet ever and always I am tempted by the hiss of *What's the use?* Still, I don't give up. Nana and Popi didn't teach me how.

BUTTERFLY Q & A

And when she asked me, "What name should I give to these flowers? Yellow and white? Sun and moon? Ivory and molten gold?" I replied, "That's silly. It's just honeysuckle."

And when she asked me, "What name should I give to this scent? A perfume? An intoxication? Perfect bliss?" I replied, "That's silly. It's just honeysuckle."

But she would neither be silenced nor dismissed. "What hunger does this nectar satisfy?" she probed, and I remembered. A little girl in plaid shorts and pigtails. A small fist clutching a broken branch: leaves like the emerald tongues of panting fairy dogs. Flowers white as ivory moons, yellow as melting sunshine. Burying my nose in blossoms. In a whirling, swirling, reeling, spinning universe of sweet, of good, of happy. Besotted with it. Addled with it. Then the wondrous anticipation of a further, an attainable, an ineluctable joy: one pinch on a pale green stopper. The triumphal tug. The ambrosial droplet.

"What hunger does this nectar satisfy?" she repeated, and I thought hard. It wasn't that the pleasure was forbidden – my father had showed me how, after all. Once. Twice. Then he forgot. Moved on to what he thought was more important business, the weighty worries of his grown-up world. But I foraged at the edge of the woods, tippling honeysuckle, a task vastly superior to any my father might accomplish. Even then I knew what really mattered, with a conviction as sure and delicious as the liquor I imbibed.

Carl Linnaeus gave honeysuckle its botanical genus, *lonicera*. Carl Linnaeus also called the butterfly the *imago*, Latin for 'image' or 'likeness.' It's not the stubborn, taciturn egg nor the voracious caterpillar nor the shrewd and secretive pupa hidden in its silky cocoon that defines what the adult of the species can aspire to, no. It's a high-flying, free-wheeling, winged beauty that is the image and likeness of the creature's mature form.

Now she wants to move on to another subject, demanding to know what holiday we Americans celebrate in the month of July. When I say, "Independence Day," she asks, "What does this mean?" I glibly respond, "Freedom," thinking she'll be satisfied, but no, she is repeating her earlier question, "What hunger does this nectar satisfy?"

I'm stumped. I've never thought of freedom as a food, but then, I've been grown up for so long I've forgotten what the adult of the human species should aspire to. I've mistaken stubborn, voracious and shrewd for mature, disregarding the high-flying, free-wheeling beauty in whose image and likeness we were made. It's a whirling, swirling universe of sweet, of good, of happy, after all, and I'm wondering if what we've been calling the American Dream all this time is now a silky, too-tight cocoon?

Only a question. Maybe I'll ask her about it, if she ever comes back. I hope she hasn't decided she has more important things to do, because if she laughs and says, "That's silly," I'll be really upset.

BERRIES, BLOSSOMS, BUNTING

So I walk the shore, picking up fragments of my scattered self – a feather, a shell, a knobbly piece of driftwood. Earth, sea, sky. The tri-weave basket that holds us all. Three strands braided to bind us. A trinity indwelling anyone dwelling on this planet.

At least, I think this explains it. Why I snatch at each object as if it were some crucial clue in a mystery I must solve. A wave-scrubbed shell; a cast-off feather; a useless chard of wood; a solitary, beach-combing woman – nithings in a vast universe, all, and yet each flames forth with a singular and urgent beauty.

At least, I think this explains it. Why it pleases me to see my own sandy footprints mixed in with the tattered hieroglyphs of bird tracks. Why I cried, yesterday, over the turtle which had wandered into my minuscule back yard. There, he'd be safe, but have no ready access to food and water, so I let him go in the thin strip of woods behind my house. There, he'd be free to seek what he needs to live, but his life would be in constant peril from the steady stream of cars into a nearby parking lot. There were no good choices left for that turtle.

At least, I think this explains it. Why it bothered me so much when the flags and bunting for July 4th went up in Walmart right after Memorial Day, and as soon as the Independence Day weekend passes, back-to-school items will appear along with clearance sales and fall clothes. Summer, it seems, is one month long now. We're more firmly tethered to marketing cycles than to nature's cycle of seasons.

At least, I think this explains it. Why I've been keeping such a vigilant watch on those blackberry bushes. The shy green blush. The profligate cascades of flowers. The brown tatters of petals clinging to a tight green knob. Then a rust-colored blush, a pristine virgin red, a ripe black purpled with juice and promise. I'll stay sentinel throughout the coming months. Walmart will be decorated for Christmas when emerald leaves turn topaz and birds finish off those berries. Just as the naked stems settle into their snow-blanketed beds, Walmart will be urging us to buy next spring's fashions.

And that explains it. Why most of us teeter through life unbalanced, on edge, anxious, like overworked donkeys chasing carrots-on-sticks. Forget the tri-weave basket of earth, sea and sky that contains us in a slow, unfolding now. Packaging, marketing and sales, that's the braid that binds us fast to an uneasy if, then, when.

On July 4, 1776, the 13 colonies declared their independence from an oppressive regime that impinged on "life, liberty and the pursuit of happiness." That was freedom's first flowering, like the cascades of springtime blossoms on blackberry bushes. Our understanding of freedom has ripened over the years: slavery is wrong, stealing land from indigenous people is wrong. One day we'll be able to pluck freedom's sweet, sustaining fruit: war itself is wrong. Meanwhile, we need to declare our independence from an oppressive regime of commercialization that has us wandering around like that turtle I found yesterday. To provide for ourselves by destroying our connection to the natural world is no good choice at all.

So here, take my osprey feather. Its shaft is called a rachis. Fused to that are branches called barbs, but you don't need to know that to call my feather beautiful, its graceful arc all mottled brown and white.

Take my oyster shell. It could be washed up from Miocene era sediment, some 20 million years old. You'll love its gleaming patina: cameo pink, dove gray, lucent copper. And the way it curves so perfectly into the palm of your hand, you'll enjoy that, as well.

Take my long, thin, crooked stick of driftwood, sanded smooth as silk by the bay. Salt and time have stained its grain into ink-dark, wavelike whorls. It would be easy to fall into those eddying depths, don't you think?

Take all my little trinkets; you'll need them. As we walk time's wave-lapped shore, picking up remnants of our scattered Self.

THE GATHERING

Plucking apples one by one, to make cider in the wooden press. Above a leafy green fretwork, the ripening moon hangs in a late afternoon sky. A mockingbird scolds from its rooftop perch, and in the garden, fat bees trundle from one blossom to the next, collecting nectar to make honey in their secret, mysterious press. If I had wings, I, too, could drone contentedly about my task, but these two arms will have to do, so I hum softly to myself. It feels good to be nestled within earth's two great wings of morning and evening, a day much like all the others yet unique unto itself, simultaneously unremarkable and unrepeatable.

With my friends away, their homestead is my responsibility these next few hours. In the barn, I trade a five gallon bucket filled with apples for a stack of empty, half-pint berry boxes, and stop to watch the swallows flit from beam to beam in endless pursuit of their insect meal. My trek back to the garden is enlivened by the darting shimmer of dragonflies, also hunting insect prey, and I remember a story I read once, long ago, about dragonflies, those harbingers of change. Born of water, maturing into air, living their short, magical lives with an exuberant joy we might all do well to imitate in our own ephemeral existence.

The blackberries are heavy with sunshine. They smell purple, they taste purple, they stain my fingers purple, and tomorrow, someone will buy them at the store and take this sweet purple sunshine home to eat. I pray that their meal will somehow include the lacy filigree of blackberry leaves, gold-stippled in this early evening light. And the eager squash vines hauling themselves upwards on the fruit-laden arc of blackberry branches bending to touch the earth. And the elegiac cooing of the doves. And the cloud-scarves draped so elegantly across sky's azure shoulders, gauzy wisps of white, of pink, of lavender, of gray.

Yes, evening is coming on now. The sheep are bleating in the field, crowded together by the gate which I'll unlatch so they can rush into the warm arms of the waiting barn. I'll round up the chickens, and herd the turkeys into their roosts. Soft clucks and muted gobbles will form the words of this night's lullaby, set to the pleated pulsing of crickets and frogs, punctuated by the haphazard strobe of fireflies, as darkness settles on the homestead like a broody hen's extended wing.

My friend, the homesteader, will rise before dawn tomorrow, to lead the sheep out, to let the chickens and turkeys run free, and I shall, no doubt, be dreaming still as I dart about on wings that blossom from azure shoulders, feathers all pink and white and lavender and gray, gathering a sweet and secret nectar from each and every task. And who's to say it isn't real food, real drink? Who would dare to call it merely magical, this meal? This joyful, this ephemeral, this sacred, this unremarkable, unrepeatable day.

◎ ◎ ◎

MIMOSA MOMENT

The blooms made me stop, the scent made me linger, the buds made me wonder about almost everything.

I know, I know, it isn't fair. You're already asking, Who, what, where? When, how, why?

Let's start over.

It was sometime in July. All the roads were lined with effervescence of mimosa. Flowers like fans, ballerinas, balloons, butterflies, I couldn't help myself, I had to get up close to one, so I parked my car on a grassy knoll, scrambled over a ditch, up a hill, into a whorl of scent as delicate as pink cobwebs, as fragile as blushing soap bubbles, I thought, How is it I have lived so long burdened by gravity when all along a nirvana of weightlessness has been waiting for me, disguised as a simple perfume?

I plucked one gossamer blossom. Tickled my cheek into a fuzzy giggle with it. Painted the flesh of one arm incandescent with a fairy brush of it. I couldn't fathom how something so small and gentle could grip my heart like a strong fist. Could make me want to pitch a tent. Spend the rest of my life there, a devotee of Mimosa.

I would sleep at night on green feathers, under a blanket soft as sunrise. Every morning I would wake, ready to go out and preach Mimosa to our harsh, our strident, our dog-eat-dog, survival-of-the-fittest, looking-out-for-number-one world. Billions of people would convert to Mimosa, coining new phrases for old values like tenderness and compassion. We would abandon force as a path to change and learn the power of cooperation, but as I stepped up to the podium to accept my Nobel Peace Prize, a bumblebee landed on an eye-level branch, and that's when I noticed the buds.

Tight green knobs, impenetrable verdigris knots, solid, infrangible nodes from which nothing could emerge and yet, from each hard pebble an effusion of soft threads had burst. A silky, extravagant testament to the unlikely. As astonishing a witness to surprising potential as pink cobwebs of morning spun from the black silk of night.

That was July, this is August. Just passing, the season for mimosa, and just passing, a woman I know, who would have become a dear friend except the impenetrable knot of sickness claimed her first. The last time I saw her, she lay in bed stroking her cat's white fur with fingers thin as twigs. The trees beyond her bedroom window seemed to reach in and stroke us both, a peaceful, consoling moment, and although she is leaving behind the pebble of her body, I know her soul will blossom into a surprise of potential.

Religion wants to teach us there is life after death. Wants to teach us tenderness and compassion as well. Most of us seem not to have learned those lessons, so maybe after all we should all convert to Mimosa, which proclaims what it also proves: that just beyond the hard, tight bud of the present, an extravagant and improbable future awaits. Amen.

AUTUMN

PREQUEL TO 'AUTUMN'

Outside? Pearl white clouds in a sapphire sky. Inside? A room full of women galumphing through our jazzercise routine in maladroit imitation of our agile teacher. We were executing some sequence, the name of which I never did catch, but: two steps to the right and forward. Twist, turn. Two steps to the left, back, twist, turn, meanwhile: arms extended at the shoulder, down, cross at the waist, up. Out, down, cross, up, out, down, then: from that dither of flopping legs and flapping arms I glance out the window to see: a single black crow streak upward into the lapis lazuli air.

Autumn, with its shifting winds and changing angle of light, seems to me to be the season that reminds us to celebrate the overarching sky, the encompassing air. Tomorrow, or the next day, or the next, whenever the river's surface is roughened by frills of whitecaps, I'll drive over to my favorite beach and watch the windsurfers. They will stand in waist-deep water, braving the increasing cold. They will manhandle stiff plastic sails into an upright position, then wait. Patiently. To catch that gust which will speed them along for an exhilarating moment they will share with the wind-borne gulls banking effortlessly overhead.

For me, the sky is shorthand for all that is beyond our reach or grasp. Unparalleled freedom. Inimitable grace. Earth is our home. The sea, well, eons ago, that was home, too, but the sky? It is the uncharted territory into which we long to fling ourselves, into which we cannot venture. Oh, sure, we have our airplanes and space shuttles, our satellites, our radar. We can track, we can trespass, but we can never belong, only awkwardly imitate that which does belong, by virtue of physiognomy or placement or ephemeral nature. I guess that's why I love to write about birds and butterflies, clouds and stars, light, sound, the scented air. I experience these as messengers that shuttle back and forth from where I am to where I might like to be, from what I am to what I might wish to become.

The sky is also a blue disguise for a black abyss, the empyrean heights, the vaulted heavens. Beyond what I see is a vastness that exceeds anything I can possibly imagine. Countless stars, each a sun for orbiting planets. Whirling concatenations of solar systems, swirling congregations of galaxies. The universe, they say, is 92 billion light years in diameter.

That number makes no sense to me, but it pleases me greatly to think that these reflections might pass on to you – from an infinite source – a tiny, tangible tingle. They begin with a meditation on the meaning of Labor Day, a holiday which, for many of us, marks the transition from summer to fall.

THE WORK WE DO*

Today they call it Flag Ponds Nature Park, but yesterday – some 12 million years ago – it was an ocean where sharks hunted and whales met to give birth and yesterday – some fifty years ago – it was a Chesapeake Bay harbor where watermen fed their families by catching fish in pound-nets to sell in Baltimore and yesterday – just a week ago – it was a beach where a smattering of folk searched for fossils and yesterday – just 24 hours ago – two high tides brought new sand to the shore and tomorrow – maybe fifty years from now – today's beach will have turned into forest and tomorrow – maybe 12 million years from now – today's folk

* Author's note. This was written in 2007. It is hoped that today's readers might be experiencing some of the new possibilities alluded to herein.

might have no language to describe what is here, or perhaps they'll call it ocean once again, or perhaps there will be nothing left but the silence from which it all emerged.

I think too much, I know that. While all those nice people combed the beach looking intently for black triangles fallen from the mouth of a Miocene-era shark, I sat morosely in my little chair just beyond the wrack line, staring at the debris the waves had ground, grated and pulverized into an homogeneous heap of white chips, black bits and gray smithereens. Somewhere in all that rubble a treasure could be found, but I could summon neither hope nor industry in the face of such an impossible task. I left.

On the path back to the parking lot, I stopped to read the signs. I especially loved the one about the edge effect. About the shifting boundaries between beach and dune, shrub and forest habitats. About the pioneer plants. The ones that can thrive in poor, sandy soil, reclaiming for land what belonged to the sea. Struggling with it, changing it, until other, less hardy vegetation can take root in the now fertile earth.

I noodled around at the Buoy Hotel, an old shanty left over from when the pound-net fishermen would camp out, February through November every year. Such hard labor. To cut and haul 50 foot poles from the forest. To hammer them into the harbor floor, 130 to support just one net. To trap the fish, scoop them into a boat, box them up for shipping. To mend the nets, keep the boats repaired, cook for themselves in cast iron skillets, make coffee in battered tin pots, drop into sleep on rough-hewn bunks under hand-made quilts, the day's work sweetened by dreams of hearth and home.

Back at the Visitor Center, I studied display cases filled with sand dollars, coral, leaf imprints, crocodile teeth, dolphin ear bones, sting ray dental plates, whale vertebrae, bones, petrified wood and Piscataway Indian fishing weights. Jumbled together without the neat labels, those precious artifacts would collapse into an homogenous heap of white chips, black bits and gray smithereens. I confess, it frightened me. If all my yesterdays are waves that grind and grate and pulverize. If this present moment is the wrack line. How will I ever know what to cherish, what to dismiss, what to keep, what to toss aside?

Labor Day is here already. It's supposed to be a tribute to the social and economic achievement of American workers. You know. The highest standard of living, the biggest gross national product, the best form of government; ours is a country of superlatives, okay, but 37 million Americans live below the poverty level, 47 million lack health insurance. It seems to me we're living in an era of shifting boundaries, with some new, some pioneer behaviors called for if we're to avoid the fate of those men who worked at the Buoy Hotel. Today, in a tree-framed pond, you can see the derelict pilings that yesterday had been their pier, before the sand bar took over, before the encroaching thrusts of spurge and thistle. The edge effect put an end to their labor, but ours is just beginning: a birthing of new possibilities this day so that dreams of hearth and home can endure unto tomorrow.

KNOWING THE WAY BY WATER

The kayak is borrowed. I stop paddling almost as soon as I'm launched, studying the ragged edges of clouds as if they offered a map to the uncharted territory my life has become. I haven't called it home for over 40 years, but the instant I'm afloat, the molecules in my body want to align with the molecules of paddle, boat and water, reconstituting that concatenation of elements in a certain direction, towards a certain spot on a certain nearby creek where, on a certain bluff, a house once stood.

Last week's paper carried a story about a pod of whales beaching itself near the Cape of Good Hope. Hundreds of volunteers endured high winds and rough surf to try to push the creatures into open seas, but the whales kept swimming back to shore, and eventually the exhausted animals had to be shot, to prevent slow death by suffocation. No one understands such strandings. The whales could be sick, or following a confused leader, or attempting to rescue a stranded pod member sending off a distress call. Scientists think whales use magnetic fields and underwater topography to orient themselves, so a magnetic disturbance or peculiar coastline formation could bewilder them.

Now, I float amidst colored buoys and numbered channel markers, signs that mean something to someone but nothing to me. More significant is the cry of a baby osprey that scrapes the salty blue air near its twig-splayed nest. I recognize that familiar combination of morbid fear and importunate demand, and I'm tempted to turn my kayak towards the creek, the bluff, the collapsing house I keep wanting to call home, but the river's waters sparkle, and flow out to the bay, then out to the ocean, then out over the whole huge earth, so I follow the river, knowing this liquid is the united sparkling of two atoms of hydrogen and one atom of oxygen. Knowing each atom is the united sparkling of protons, neutrons, electrons. That each proton is the united sparkling of quarks and photons, each of which is a sparkling. Of. Something. That unites this kayak, this paddle, these hands that hold the paddle, the osprey's open beak, the twigs of its nest, those trees along the shore, this whole huge earth and, indeed, the universe itself. One united sparkling.

Home.

And if the old house is collapsing, I think that's a good thing. Like those whales, we've been sick, following confused leaders, attempting to rescue something that's beyond hope of repair. We all must contribute to the great work: finding a new orientation so we don't end up stranded on a deadly shore, and in this uncharted territory, maybe those drifting clouds are a map, after all, with their hydrogen and their oxygen, their quarks and their photons, those mysterious inner somethings that teach us what we already know, in our sparkling bones: that beyond morbid fear and importunate demand there is a way for this glorious concatenation of elements we call the Earth to align itself rightly and arrive home together as a single, sacred community.

BONES

Last week, I dreamt someone had hired a sky writer to send me messages. My name was writ large across the sky, followed by a private communication made available for public scrutiny. The next morning, I found bones on the path to the creek, three fist-sized vertebrae from some hapless deer that fit snugly together, like an intricate Chinese puzzle. As instructed by my dream, I inspected the individual discovery for its collective meaning, and here is what I found.

Each of our four seasons is three months long. Three is a potent number. Earth is the third planet from the sun. Plato thought the world was built from that three-sided shape, the triangle, and he wasn't far wrong, because the atomic foundation of the universe is, in fact, triune: protons, neutrons, electrons. Babylonians had three primary gods representing Heaven, Earth and the Abyss. Christians have the Blessed Trinity. Not to mention, three billy goats gruff, three witches in *Macbeth*, and the standard three wishes every genie grants to its liberator.

From three I moved on to other patterns. I saw five ospreys orbiting each other like a feathered galaxy. Puckered sand in the shallow breakwater looked like the crimped mountains and valleys of Appalachia, not surprising, since currents of wind and water and time created both. I noticed how shrinkage patterns make identical crazing on ceramics, dried-out paint or parched earth. How certain crystalline formations echo the mind-teasing structure of a labyrinth.

Curious, I went into research mode. In the Chinese language, there is a word, *li*. The character for *li* represents the markings in jade, the grain in wood, the fiber in muscle. *Li* means the dynamic forms at work in nature, great families of structure that repeat in many manifestations.

Aggregations, branches, fractures, ripples will cause similar patterns in bark, soap, marble, galaxies, on an animal's skin or within the secret architecture of cells.

Li is also a spiritual concept. When you're centered, when you're in accord with the Tao, you move through life with the same ease as dancing waves, which are like wafting clouds, which are like flickering flames. Your soul mirrors nature's dynamic harmonies, the forces at work in trees, rivers, stars and the secret architecture of the human heart.

Yesterday, I fell asleep on the beach. The wind scripted its fluent alphabet in the leaves, on my skin, across the water's ruffled surface. Consciousness flickered, images wafted, as spontaneous and unpredictable as which combinations of hydrogen and oxygen will froth up into what dancing wave.

Now, the autumnal equinox. One season becoming another. The bones of the year interlocking with fish bones, dinosaur bones, the scattered bones of planetary nebulae. Some great organism rising from the muck of the universe.

Animal, mineral and vegetable. Thinking our thoughts, dreaming our dreams, waking from our sleep to dance, to waft, to flicker through our private and public memories, scribbling messages from us to the future.

If I could read those letters, I would share them with you.

A SLOW AND GENTLE EASING

What if we don't call it death? What if we call it a slow and gentle easing into what follows, and take, for teacher, this season of autumn? This began for me long before it began, way back in August, with one anomalous yellow leaf falling at my sandal-clad feet. Then, days later, another. Then, days later, a quick trip across the bridge, with a swath of treetops spread out below me, green whispering rumors of buried gold.

In that instant I became autumn's hunter, on the alert for signs of my still-elusive prey. Subtle changes in the slant of light. Night's small, inexorable inroads into day. A gradual crisping of the air, mind and body grateful for their release from summer's hot, wet embrace. The equinox came. The flat open palms of some leaves closed up into little silver fists, as if to grab and keep whatever had been theirs for whatever little while. Other leaves surrendered to color, to splotches of topaz, saffron, scarlet. Stains of eggplant purple, claret red, doeskin brown. The river turned blue. Pumpkins appeared in the fields, and corn stubble. Marigolds sprouted along walkways where brittle leaves scraped in every gust of wind.

Hunter no longer, that which I sought now avidly seeks me. Around any corner I can jump onto some dizzying carousel of color. Goodbye to the staid and stalwart greens of summer. Hello to paisleys, plaids, checks, stripes. Stippled, smeared, sprayed and splashed all across the countryside. If I grabbed some tree and asked it to explain, it would say, "Making food from sunlight is harder than you think, I'm just all tuckered out. My leaves are damaged anyhow, all those insects and diseases. I've sent out some hormones, they're making a wall between my leaves and my twigs. Without water, the green chlorophyll will disintegrate and, presto-change-o, pigments invisible all summer will magically appear: orange carotenes, yellow xanthophylls, red phycoerythrins. I'll need to store up every last bit of sugar, so I'll manufacture some anthocyanin. That will turn the glucose remnants purple, and when there's nothing left but waste products, the tannin will turn brown, the wind will carry the last of the leaves away and then, finally, I can rest."

Okay, teach, I've got it, straight from the horse's mouth. The world is falling asleep. Slipping from wakefulness into dreams. Losing its grip on the workaday business of productivity, turning to the necessary task of renewal. I wish I had time for that, but I've got people coming over for the holidays. Then I have to get famous so I can get rich, I don't want to die alone. I wouldn't be alone except for all these worn out behaviors, but they've been mine for so long, it's hard to believe things could be different. Trees have new leaves inside them somewhere. After all this dying, a season of fresh growth is bound to follow, but me, I can't afford the risk, and what would I dream about anyhow?

RAINDROPS IN THE RIVER

It rained, briefly, then stopped, then started again. I thought, No need to dash for cover, this isn't going to last long. And stayed put. On the beach. Listening to raindrops behind me: tat, tat, tat on the stiff marsh grass, like tiny claws. Feeling raindrops on my face: tat, tat, tat on soft, warm flesh, insistent, a drum roll. Watching raindrops on river's surface, her face pocked and cratered. Tat: one drop plunges to its death. Tat: melts into concentric circles. Tat: lives again as flowing water. Tat, tat, tat.

By the time I got back to where my car waited – up the hill I clambered, into the woods I plunged, along the leaf-caked path I ambled – by this time I am softened. Tat, tat, tat. Ready to vanish. Tat, tat, tat. Melt into something else.

Now the rain stops. Silence. "Hush," the trees whisper, "Mum's the word." I touch my lips, checking, yes, they're all buttoned up. Thoughts are another matter. I do my best to let them melt, tat, tat, tat, into the thought-river flowing in my pocked and cratered brain.

I glance down. There's a ditch along the side of the road, clotted with leaves, filled with water. Dead leaves in a ditch, I think, but no, my brain registers a mighty fretwork of yellow and red and orange trees towering loftily, no, plunging down into sky to where gray clouds drift by, billowing underfoot, no, drifting high above, no, heaped in roiling masses and submerged beneath the swaying treetops that are reflected in the fathomless depths of a shallow roadside ditch.

I trace and retrace my steps, lost in the confounding shift between illusion and reality. If I stare at the leaves, the reflection vanishes. How mundane. Clouds above if I crane my neck, yes, a bit of fringed treetop, okay, myriads of gray trunks bristling in the forest, if I glance off to the side, ho-hum.

But when I gaze at the reflection, a dizzying panorama reveals itself, whole and complete. A majesty of multihued trees soaring together into a vast and infinite sky. Not the tat, tat, tat of separate entities, but the flowing river, and which is really real, I ask myself, and then I laugh out loud. "My me is God," said Catherine of Genoa some 500 years ago, "Nor do I recognize any other me except my God."

I'm still laughing now, as I write, because the moment was so vivid, so profound, and now it's vanished, and I'm stuck here trying to explain it. Something about me: a shallow, leaf-clogged ditch. Something about God: vast, infinite, contained by, containing all. Something about seeing the one reflected in the other, and something from my college psych class. About figure-ground relationships. Is it a vase or two faces? Is it a rabbit or a duck? Is it me, or God? Is it God-in-me or me-in-God? The whole is different than the sum of its parts.

I guess I have a choice, what I want to attend to, moment by moment, day by day, the figure or the ground. Because one way, it's just, tat, tat, tat, drops of rain, dying. Another way, it's deep calling to deep, tat, tat, tat, in a mighty river, melting.

FOSSILS

Arriving, I am greeted by their arrival, as they, in turn, are greeted by the shore. Kiss, kiss, kiss, say the waves, falling onto outstretched arms of sand. Home at last and welcome, after such a journey.

I know how they feel. It was just a two mile hike to get here, and yet I passed through epochs, startling thrush in the color-drenched, autumnal forest, herons in the marsh, and now, gulls spiral up and away as I look across the Chesapeake Bay from this beach at Calvert Cliffs.

I am a pilgrim. Sent by I don't know whom, to find I don't know what, but already kind strangers have equipped me for the task. That first woman along the way. She was trudging back to the parking lot with two tired children. I was aiming for the beach, wondering what a shark's tooth looks like, how on earth one hunts for fossils, and fossils of what, by the way. Because dawn tugged me from sleep this morning. Whispered a word in my ear. I'd heard about this place and so – obedient, expectant, trusting – I came. At a fallen tree I met her, each of us scrambling over in our opposite directions. A smile, a greeting, a conversation on the path. She described shark teeth. Gave me her daughter's sieve so I could sift for them among the pebbles.

Then that young man. He and I, both first timers, both holding our shoes, both puzzling over where to leave them. He had prepared for his visit with research, and gave me a crash course in regional paleontology. I shared with him my *chutzpah*, boldly suggesting we put our shoes together under the closest tree. Barefoot, we parted. He has disappeared around the bend already while I stand here, mesmerized.

My new friend told me that some 20 million years ago, Southern Maryland was covered by a warm, shallow sea. These cliffs that tower some 60 feet above me are the sand, silt and clay that settled on that ancient ocean floor, burying and preserving an amazing variety of Miocene-era fauna. Marine animals, mostly – sharks, rays, whales, seals, crocodiles – but bone fragments from mastodons, wooly rhinos and even camels have been discovered. Shells and shark teeth predominate, because they're hard already, more easily fossilized, and because they're abundant. A single shark will shed some ten thousand teeth in its lifetime, and mollusks are the sparrow of the undersea world: over 400 species of clam, oyster, scallop and snail have been identified here.

"What makes a fossil, anyway?" I asked him, and he happily obliged with an explanation. Scientists call it 'permineralization.' Water infused with minerals passes through the decaying object, substituting calcite, iron or silica for the original chemicals. Over millions of years the artifact is completely replaced. What remains is a rock-like copy. And here comes Elizabeth, soft flesh stretched over hard bone, a fossil hominid in the making, one day to be discovered along with her borrowed tool. Or not. Most life disappears without a trace, too fragile to endure into such a memorial. Like those soldiers whose faces I see daily in the paper. Killed when a makeshift bomb exploded. Shot by snipers. Struck by shrapnel. Beheaded.

After a few tries at the water's edge, I abandon my sieve. Poking through 10,000 round pebbles to find one triangular shark's tooth is a task far exceeding my need to find such a prize, and I'm distracted by the lure of other treasures. Color, for one. Right at my feet, in countless shells and rocks. Gray like iron, like steel, like storm clouds. Black like tar, like smoke, like twilight. The browns of chocolate, toast, a fawn's dappled back, blended in with cameo pinks, pumpkin oranges. Three steps down the beach, and now the rocks are ebony smears and henna washes; the shells lucent copper, nacreous tea rose. Old already when the Palagornis flew, that extinct pelican with its 18 foot wingspan. Old already when the Megatooth shark swam, 50 feet long, weighing in at 50 tons.

I bend down and snatch from this 21st century beach an artifact washed up from 20 million years ago. By shape, by size, by mother-of-pearl glints: an oyster shell. Yet pitted with holes like stone, gnarled like arthritic bone, its colors faded to cotton white: this thing is on its way to becoming something else. As is this tree stump, turned on water's lathe into the very shape of sea spume. And these hulking rocks, printed all over with shell shapes, primordial mollusks stamped into earth's sealing wax. From the cliffs above me the boulders have tumbled, sediment from a Miocene ocean floor, changed into stone, returning to a Chesapeake beach to be chiseled by today's waves into tomorrow's sandy shore. Faithful Penelope. Day by day and year by year the bay's fingers of swash and backwash pluck at this palisade, unraveling an adamantine cloth woven by time.

Squatting at the base of the embankment, looking up, I count at least 10 distinct seams of shell deposits, each in its uniquely colored strata of clay or sandstone. The cliff face is a multi-layered cake, topped with a green woodsy frosting.

but it's crumbling away even as I sit here, pelting me with bits of prehistoric earth. I've heard it said that one day, all secrets will be shouted from the housetops, and peering closely at a fallen chunk of sediment from the bottom of some primal sea, I think this must be true. I run my fingers along the blurred edges of shells, buried eons ago, now straining to escape their tomb. They thrust up, eagerly waiting for the one wave that will at last set them free.

As do we all, on our way to becoming something else.

Earth is 4.5 billion years old. Without making any far-fetched claim for algae, it seems pretty obvious that consciousness and matter have made some profuse and colorful blendings along the way. Single celled, multi-celled, with nervous systems simple or complex, organisms keep evolving. Reptiles, fish, birds, mammals, and now, beings through whom the universe can think about itself. Over millennia, minerals replace chemicals, hard bone turns to fossil rock. Spirit infuses matter, we share experience, pass it on, ask questions, draw conclusions, make decisions. Awareness grows. We change. If some dead soldier of today should turn up a million years hence clutching a weapon, might it be to the kind of fanfare with which we greeted the discovery of *Australopithecus afarensis*? Kiss, kiss, kiss for a forerunner of modern human?

I am for home now, pilgrimage complete for this one day at least. The wind that brings these waves to brush against my feet could have brushed against the face of some stranger on a far distant shore. A smile, a greeting, a conversation on the path, we don't know what awaits us. As I stoop to retrieve my shoes, an acorn falls from a high above branch, its sharp fresh green a surprise on the pale brown sand. I'm tempted to pocket it as a souvenir, but no, this seed bears within itself the gift of its own future. I guess I owe it one small chance.

VIGIL

I waited. High up in the Smokies, where mist curls from the treetops like steam in a hot green cauldron. Where clouds stack up like mountains, and mountains roll away like clouds, rippling to the horizon in an undulating current of hill and vale, high and low, a pulse as regular as wingbeats, up and down, a vertical in-ing and out-ing, like the tide.

I waited. On the first night, dark blue cloud-tongs opened briefly, letting fall to earth a glowing ember of sun, but I saw no stars. On the second night, the clabbered clouds parted long enough to reveal a pearl white moon on a nacreous chip of pink sky-shell, but I saw no stars. On the third night, I rose at midnight, peering past black lace leaves onto an unfurling bolt of ebony velvet. From tree to tree I heard the antiphonal chant of crickets and frogs, but I saw no stars.

Six nights I waited. Flesh of my flesh, I thought, bone of my bones. Elemental ovens, where carbon, nitrogen and oxygen were synthesized, released, refashioned, relinquished, formed all over again then set free to make all the planets and every manner of thing inhabiting them. Billions of years up and down, infinity's wingbeats, billions of years in and out, a cosmic tide. How I longed to see them, my an-cestors, my companions, my guides. Six nights I waited, and on the seventh day, it was time to come home, where artificial light has long since replaced starshine in the nighttime sky.

The word 'vigil' means 'awake, alert, watchful.' There are formal times set aside for such watchfulness – on the eve of special festivals or holy days. There are times when life makes spontaneous demands of alertness from us – at the bedside of a sick child, a dying friend. On the eve of Yom Kippur, the Jewish holy day celebrated in autumn, the congregation prays, "May all the people of Israel be forgiven, including the strangers who live in their midst, for all the people are at fault."

When I was in North Carolina, I kept my evening vigils, praying to see the stars. By day I drove on steep narrow roads through a thick cloth woven from sunlight and shade, embroidered with the sounds of birds and insects. I drove through the V-shaped folds, up and down, in and out, thinking of the Cherokee people who had lived in those mountains for 10,000 years, until, coveting what belonged to others by virtue of ancestral gift, the strangers living in their midst claimed the land as their own. Back into the thick cloth that is Southern Maryland, my pen stitches the names of the people who lived here for 10,000 years – Patuxents, Piscataways, Nanjemoys, Mattapanys, Wicomicoes, Portopacos, Mattawomans, Chapticos – until we took the land they lived on, and their inheritance became ours.

Now we celebrate Columbus Day. Guided by the stars, Columbus made his voyage of discovery and stumbled on this continent. The stars guide us still, for tomorrow's new world is today being synthesized in the elemental ovens of all the peoples' hearts. Flesh of my flesh, bone of my bone, we are learning to say to each other, to our Earth. Everyone at fault, everyone forgiven, everyone set free to begin a new voyage of discovery that will take us, not out, but in.

Shall we acknowledge that life on this planet is making a spontaneous demand of alertness from us? Shall we begin our vigil now? In the great cycles of day and night, there is a light appropriate to every work: the sun for growing up, the moon and stars for growing down. Tonight, as our eyes flutter closed and darkness covers the waters of our sleep. As all thinking and desiring melt away. Let us pray for something deeper than thought or desire: that Earth's own wanting will take hold of us, that the Earth's own dream for herself will take shape within us. So that tomorrow, as our eyes flutter open, we can say, "Let there be light."

BAKING FOR THE HOLIDAYS

"Lay me down like a stone, raise me up like bread." As prayers go, this one's a champ, don't you think? I picked it up from a character in Tolstoy's *War and Peace* some thirty years ago. Still murmur it at night before drifting off into sleep, that dark oven that bakes us new again each morning.

Yes, and it's October already. Time to prepare for winter's dark oven. Time to befriend the night. From my deck I see her stride towards me, earlier each evening: arms outstretched, palms held open in surrender and supplication. From my deck I listen to her song: the stars and the crickets, a soprano of vast distances, an alto of all that is near and dear, yes, it is good to get to know this woman, darkness, for isn't she our mother? It seems so, at dusk, when lengthening shadows hurry to the solace of her breast. Or at dawn, when all things reluctantly depart the refuge of her silhouette.

Out in space, the sky is always black, for there's no atmosphere, no dust or gas molecules to absorb or reflect light's waves. Out in space, it's always silent, for there's no medium through which sound's waves can travel. Out in space, it's almost always cold, the objects that could conduct or radiate heat so few, so far between. Out in space is where our Earth is planted, who could forget it, with cold dark silent winter coming on?

Yesterday I woke up earlier than the sun. From my deck I watched night's beloved, inmost mystery become tangible in the day's affairs. As an incoming tide of light submerged the stars like pebbles on a beach, all the known and familiar configurations emerged: bird calls and traffic and a laughing child, the comforting evidence of routine and rational thought. Yet when I went to the store, it was magic and unreason that overflowed the aisles in festoons of orange and black.

We call it Halloween, but for the ancient Celts it was *Samhain*, 'summer's end.' Their New Year began with winter on November 1st, so October 31st was their New Year's Eve, a moment outside of time when the natural order of the universe dissolved back into primordial chaos before righting itself again. The dead could walk the earth that night, their strange and otherworldly soprano blending with our close, familiar alto.

"Lay me down like a stone, raise me up like bread." As prayers go, this one's perfect for the season. First comes Halloween, that riotous, phantasmagoric celebration of everything we fear and can't understand. That should soften us up a bit. Next comes cozy Thanksgiving. No need to fret the constant plunge through cold dark silent space, because Thanksgiving's warm and loving hands will knead us.

Finally, winter's long sleep. May we go in as dough, spirit and flesh. Come out next spring, body and soul newly risen. And if anybody asks, please say you picked up that prayer from me.

JOE'S GARDEN

At the party, Joe's table contribution was two grocery sacks stuffed with salad greens, cucumbers, carrots and radishes, which I ignored when filling my plate because I hate cold crunchy food. But everywhere I turned that night, there was Joe, talking about his produce with the enthusiasm of a first-time astronaut just back from a stroll on the moon. "I want to see your garden," I said, and that's how I, maven of the frozen entree, ended up at Joe's place last week.

I hear us now. Me, giggling. Joe's voice, exuberant. "Look at this," he exclaims, "Chinese Red Meat Radish." He whips out his pocket knife and slices into the white roundness. "It's magenta inside, have you ever seen anything so beautiful?" I murmur an appreciative "No," and Joe continues, "It tastes every bit as good as it looks, sweet, crisp, great for stir-fries, and over here." He points up the row, "German Heirloom Radish, more pungent." Tenderly brushing back the mounded dirt, he sighs, "See that green shoulder? And this." I hold my breath to the silent drum roll. "Black Spanish Radish." Triumphant, he holds aloft a verdant sheaf from which dangles an ebony globe. "Grated, sliced, raw, fabulous with lentil soup," he boasts. I make a sound I hope is sufficiently admiring of such versatility.

Over the next hour we will wend our way up and down the long rows, where every plant took seed first in Joe's heart and he knows them as a mother knows the children of her womb. With him I will rave over the collard leaves, which look like some flower's wild, green dream. I will wrinkle my brow, wondering, Will that tiny cabbage make it before first frost?

Joe's friend, Mike, is in the far field, plucking kale to make Southern Maryland stuffed ham for Thanksgiving. Joe will call out, "Make sure you get some broccoli, it's absolutely gorgeous!" He will stoop down, straighten, place a rock in my open palm. "Part of the beauty of gardening here," he says. "This land was settled long before we arrived." The rock is triangular, knapped to a sharp point, notched at the broad end. My forefinger curls into the groove, brain slowly registering what hand had instantly learned: a fine digging tool.

It smells like the dirt it came from, seed-like promise of something both urgent and unfathomable. Shaped like a heart? A womb? I imagine I am the ancestor who wielded it, readying my store of implements for spring, which will be long in the coming but the season of growth will arrive, and from planting to harvest I will know, even as I am known: a unique and irreplaceable beauty. Worthy of love and admiration.

And if this is what we all want, isn't this also what we could give birth to? The whole world to be our carefully tended, our bounteous, our infinitely diverse, oh-so versatile and generously shared garden?

Maybe I'll meet you at the party.

THANKSGIVING REVERIE

On any map, St. Mary's County, Maryland is clearly a peninsula formed by three rivers and the Chesapeake Bay. But it's not the map that makes it ours, this land, this peninsula, this long, narrow trestle table heavy laden with such rich and bounteous fare. It's that we come to the table to sup together on what, together, we have been given.

The gift of water. Like silver or silk or tumbling jazz notes. In diamond dashes or foam-flecked tiers. In sheets of lead, on cloudy days, or pocked and roughened by some storm.

The gift of sky. How legion, those blues: azure, cerulean, cornflower, Wedgwood, robin's egg, sapphire. How changeable, those clouds:

wisps, tatters, billows, or even, at sunset, carnelian paving stones.

The gift of earth, whether carefully cultivated (lawn, field, rose arbor) or wild and profuse (thick woods, ivy-clotted cliffs, leaping deer).

In college, our class read "Ode on a Grecian Urn" by John Keats. I clearly remember scoffing at those famous last two lines: "'Beauty is truth, truth beauty,' – that is all/Ye know on earth, and all ye need to know." How stupid, I thought. How can people say this guy's a great poet, I wondered, when he's foisting nonsense off on us like something we can rely on?

I was young, and angry. I wanted life to make sense – it didn't. I wanted certainty – none could be found. Keats' words disappointed me, epitomizing all the broken promises and frustrated hopes the world had so far proffered, so I marched off to find a more substantial truth.

Flash forward. This current November day. I'm walking somewhere, and I'm startled by the vivid purple tips of a seed-blown thistle flower. Or maybe I'm driving, and the shape of a drifting cloud catches me off-guard. Or I'm sitting in my back yard, and some bird pipes up with a burst of song, and for one instant I'm freed from my tiny self's illusory baggage of broken promises and frustrated hopes, catapulted to a place that's large and real and true. I need to name it, the place where I've been, so I smile and think, "O, that's beautiful."

Flash back. 1621. Plymouth, Massachusetts. A harvest festival. A handful of immigrants and native-born folk, come together to sup on what, together, they have been given. Never mind the table, heavy laden with bounteous fare; it's the place that really matters, because the beauty in which we dwell is the truth that dwells within us. It's the American Dream. It's the American challenge. It's the one thing that can take us beyond red or blue states of mind, beyond politicians' broken promises or the frustrated hopes of bogus social agendas.

Flash forward. Some future Thanksgiving Day. "O beautiful," they're singing, from sea to shining sea. The native-born and the immigrants, the black and the white, the yellow, the red, the brown folk. Poor and rich, young and old, all come together – like us, today – to give thanks for what, together, we have been given.

THANKSGIVING HALLELUJAH

Our ancestors – and I'm talking millions of years now, not just a century or two – our ancestors sat around a fire at night and told stories. Imagine. The sputtering red, hissing orange, flickering yellow. Just like now.

November. Driving down some back country road. The trees slipping out of summer's green disguise to reveal themselves as what they truly are: fire. Flames of it sputtering in the woods, sparks of it hissing onto the pavement, leaping licks of it flickering along stout limbs and spindly branches. Just like then. Imagine.

The sputtering, hissing, flickering blaze cooks your food, warms your flesh, keeps wild creatures away and is the only light you can count on to find your way in the enveloping dark. You huddle close, with others huddled close, all of you listening as one to a voice that spins the firelight into words, knits the words into images, weaves the images into a tale that reveals who you are, how you came to be here, what you can hope to accomplish before you tiptoe from the circle into the howling night. Just like now.

No painter could ever do justice to the color flaring forth from these trees, because all these tints and tones, these hues and tinges, they're not being applied to some inert canvas by some distant third party then offered up for my enjoyment, no. This moment is an intimate waltz, a sexy tango, a strut-your-stuff cha-cha-cha between me and a living essence. It is light recreating itself in leaf molecules, in eyeball molecules, light becoming a part of the tree, then becoming a part of me, then becoming conscious of itself, then rejoicing because it knows itself to be glory and praise and hallelujah.

Listen. My voice spins the leaflight into words, images, a story. Listen. In the beginning, time and space and molecules came forth from fire, a sputtering, hissing, flickering blaze of possibility and potential. Beneath this disguise of skin and bone, our living souls are still aflame.  With desire: the longing, craving, needing, demanding, wanting. With hope: believing desire can be fulfilled. Listen. It's a very long story, so I'll skip to now, Thanksgiving Day 2008, and I'll tell you what I think. No, scratch that, I'll tell you how I feel.

If I had a galaxy-sized table. If I were to place in the center of my table a cornucopia the size of the planet Earth. I would fill my trumpet-shaped basket with smiles. The smiles I saw on the faces of men, women and children all around the world, rejoicing because an African American had been elected president of the United States. I would add the sweat of all the people who came to America in chains. And the tears of the first Americans, who were driven from their land so that others could call it home. And the hidden anguish of all the trees chopped down so that concrete expressways might flourish. Then I would mix in the determination of anyone who ever arrived on these shores, having left a place where possibility seemed extinguished.

And then I would give thanks. For this amazing moment when we can gather around the living flame of our longings, cravings, needings, demandings, wantings. To tell ourselves, once again, in words and images, the story of who we are and how we came to be here. Because the American Dream is not some paint to be applied to the inert canvas of other countries around the world, no. It's an invitation. To every person on Earth. Whatever tint or tone or hue or tinge your living light of hope may be, now is the time to do an intimate waltz or a sexy tango or a strut-your-

stuff cha-cha-cha with it. Because each of us is a glory and a praise, with something important to do before we tiptoe from the circle, and together we are hallelujah, a sputtering, hissing, flickering blaze of possibility and potential. In this new beginning.

THE MOON OF MY BELONGING

Who can lay claim to the moon? Despite the footsteps imprinted in her dust and the flags hanging limp above her windless surface, the moon belongs to all humankind. So says the United Nations in a 1967 treaty which forbids individual nations from appropriating parts of the moonscape, but fails to exclude private ownership. A surprising number of people have tried to take advantage of this loophole, insisting on their right to buy, sell, swap or otherwise profit from an exchange of extraterrestrial real estate. You laugh? So did I. But then the sadness kicked in: human nature at its avaricious worst.

Quick! Make a list of book or song or movie titles with the word 'moon' in them. This chuck of lifeless rock carries our hearts and longings with her on her 28 day journey. She governs our plantings and our thievings, our emotions and our tides. Earth spins round and round. Earth's oceans spin round and round. Heaping up towards the moon, emptying out away from the moon. Increasing with her light, diminishing with her strength. High tide, low tide. Lunar push, lunar pull.

Through my lifetime I have known three moons. In New York City I could hardly find her among the street lights. Amidst the ebb and flow of traffic and ambition, what power could the moon possess?

In the high desert of northern New Mexico, the moon was sterling silver in an onyx sky. I gauged her size with words I'd formerly reserved for olives: gargantuan, colossal, mammoth. She gave me a house of baked clay. Plunked me down in a barren, cratered landscape uncannily like her own: the white sandstone of *Plaza Blanca*. Flecked with silver mica. Pocked with ancient rocks. Even at her first quarter, the very ground swelled with light. By the full, I who had once dismissed the moon learned my own insignificance.

Now I live in St. Mary's County, Maryland, which juts into the Chesapeake Bay across three rivers like a long narrow pier. The sky is a blue-black mussel shell; the moon, its mother-of-pearl glow. Rising over our rippled, wavering waters, she sees herself reflected in a thousand silver chips. Hears herself discussed in a thousand conversations between soft night breezes and sea grass, murmuring insects and creaking pines, dry leaves and prowling critters, waves and the foam-gilt shore.

This is her family. She is at home here. Her magnetic fingers twine throughout our countryside, pulling at our rivers, tugging at our creeks. At the syzygy, the new and the full, the moon's face turns directly on us and we receive the abundant spring tides. At the quadrature, when her face slants away, our neap tides are scanty. More reliable than any legal contract, these risings and fallings. A treasure continually replenishing itself. An inheritance beyond price.

Who can lay claim to the moon? In my lifetime I have known three. This last, over Southern Maryland, is the moon of my belonging. I give it to you.

THE BARN

Hushed and expectant, they await their moment of usefulness. Tillers, plows, lawn mowers, arranged by size. Rolls of chicken wire and electric fencing, neatly tied. Nestling tidily inside each other: empty buckets. Arranged on a pegboard: hammers, mallets, screwdrivers, wrenches. A level. Work gloves. Even the rowboat seems to be anticipating something, off in its corner, under its tarp. Because after all the digging and planting, the hewing and pulling and pounding, after one too many an arduous day, the tired homesteaders will turn away, briefly, from their labors. Kick back. Relax. Enjoy their row up the Potomac despite the jeers of the other boaters to "Get a motor!" Powered by nothing save muscle and purpose, the homesteaders will explore the river where fish swim and birds fly and worms churn the sediment and all things arrive where they're going, fueled only by muscle and purpose.

And where have we arrived, with our motors? With our technological advances that can take us to the nether reaches of the solar system but still can't feed the population of this planet? 50,000 children will die of hunger today because you and I like to get where we're going fast and easy. That's 100,000 parents. 500,000 brothers and sisters, aunts, uncles, grandparents. They'll all be grieving tomorrow because you and I want our food grown, packaged and even prepared by others. I'm no expert on geopolitical, geosocial, geoeconomic issues, but I do know this is true: I take up more than my fair share of this world's goods. More warmth in winter, more coolness in summer, more comfort and convenience than I'm entitled to.

I'm not lazy. I labor diligently, just like you, but I've lost touch with something vital. The barn at the homestead is red. It's a tough, hard-

-working muscle with invisible arteries fanning out into all the fields, where grass feeds the sheep, and bugs in the grass feed the chickens, and sheep and chickens feed the homesteaders, who harvest tomatoes and squash and peppers and onions, then toss what remains on the compost heap to feed the soil on which the cycle depends.

What, then of the human heart, which is more than a tough, hard-working muscle? The dictionary says love arises from recognition of attractive qualities or instincts of natural relationship, and manifests as feelings of affection, attachment; as solicitude for the beloved's welfare, delight in the beloved's presence. I don't feel this for the food I buy at Giant, do you? After she puts her animals in their stalls for the night, my friend the homesteader calls out, laughingly, "You're good sheep!" Then she goes inside to spin their wool into warm sweaters. She frets over the turkeys she must butcher, and discusses her seedlings as any proud parent might boast about a child. When I'm with her, the rafters of my heart expand. All love's tools await their moment of usefulness as, with muscle and purpose, I set myself to the task of caring for this place of my belonging, this Earth, my only and every beloved.

IN PRAISE OF SURF

At Point Lookout, Maryland, earth turns into a sharp needle, stitching St. Mary's County into the Chesapeake Bay, and all along the beach, a snaky filament of white cotton surf tries to thread itself back into the needle's eye.

These waves. Wind beating ocean's drum skin thousands of miles away, wind switching on ocean's lamplight, thousands of miles away, wind gifting itself to ocean's embrace, thousands of miles away and precisely now, the energy that was wind, precisely and exactly here, the energy gifts itself onto the shore as waves of water, tumbling, surging. As waves of sound, crashing, dashing. As waves of light, throbbing, pulsing.

These waves. Even as they leave the bay for the beach, they depart the beach to return to the bay. The simultaneity of them. Not this coming then that going, but both together, coming and going, arrival and departure, the boundary between this and that, between then and now, blurring, in the swirling surf, blurring, in the watching woman, blurring, the waves and the woman, two tines of a tuning fork, struck, reverberating as one pure note. Call it eternity, or infinity, or forever.

Or call it love. On the way down to the beach, I passed a family out for a stroll. Mother, father, child. I asked the little girl, “Are you having a nice walk?” She replied, “I love my Daddy.” I thought, Out of the mouths of babes! Love is the answer to every question, a perpetuity of give and take, the child offering to me what she received from her father, the tumbling, surging surf offering to earth what it received from air, giving back to water what it’s taking from land. A triune transmutation of energy, endless in its duration, constant in its changeableness.

Yes, call it love, the surf, and hold fast to it through your days and nights. As you wake, with salty dream-fingers still clutching the pristine sand of your barely conscious mind. As you plod to the bathroom to brush your teeth, each footfall a transmutation of energy given to the floor from your body, from yesterday's meals, last month's crops and critters, last year's sunshine, all of that now offered back to earth precisely and exactly here, in each shuffling footstep that echoes – doesn't it? – the sibilant shuffling of waves on the shore.

In all your hours, hold fast to it. In the crashing, dashing cycles of grievance and forgiveness. In the throbbing, pulsing revolutions of mistake and rectification. In the comings and goings and arrivals and departures that crest, fold in on themselves, wash up onto your experience then wash back down into your memory, the boundary between this and that, blurring in the swirling surf, the boundary between then and now blurring, in the watching soul, the surf and the soul, two tines of a tuning fork, struck, reverberating as one pure note called eternity or infinity or forever or love, until all that surging, snaky filament threads itself back into the needle's eye.

WINTER

PREQUEL TO 'WINTER'

Almost, it could be a mist, a gray cloud clinging to the earth, but no. As the road curves closer, the fog resolves itself into a tangled profusion of bare tree branches. I marvel at the work of winter: to strip green flesh from canescent bones.

The work of winter. An odd thought. Intrigued, I decide my errands can wait while I make my R.S.V.P. to this unexpected invitation. Remembering a park nearby, I head there, noting that heaven itself seems naked today: blue-gray clouds on a gray-blue sky. Despite what I know – that each season possesses its own wisdom – I've always hated winter. Have always preferred to build of its hard-packed longings something like a tower from which I could spy, in the distance, the coming spring. Now winter proffers her hand in friendship. Shall I take it?

I park my car and leave it, like some discarded garment. I need to be naked. Exposed. Like the trees themselves. The path I choose – or is it chosen for me? – takes me deep into the woods. Or is this the framework of a house being built? So many questions, so few answers, and that, too, is the work of winter, I suspect. To strip away the green flesh of our assumptions, taking us down to the bare bones of perplexity. The framework of a life being built. Of many lives being fashioned from puzzle and inquiry. The house that is the life of the world.

This forest, now, is the gray realm of burnt things: ash, charcoal, cinder. Of hard, metallic things: iron, steel, granite, lead. And yet, something is revealed here that hitherto had been hidden. Just there, in the serpentine twist of a limb, the rope-like curve of a bough, the surprise of twigs flaring forth from the tip of that branch, like fingers on a groping hand. And there, in the bold lines or brazen angles of trunks straight or bent. I can see what living has done to each tree; I can see, in consequence, every storm, every wind, every drought. Good season, bad season. Accident, happy chance. I can see it all, and I am here to tell you this: it is all beautiful.

Deep calls to deep, the psalm says. In this skeletal wood, my own soul's bones expose themselves: the choices I've made, my mistakes, my regrets. Yet the marrow of me knows what the cold sap knows: the fundamental architecture of any life is beautiful. All our leanings and all our twistings, our fits and starts, our strides and missteps, it's all a hidden magnificence. Even when choice has been taken from us – through brutal storm or harsh accident – even then, something beautiful is being built. One life. Many lives. The house that is the life of the world.

I return to car and errands, startling a flock of small birds: black pepper swirling to spice a gray sky. I have clasped winter's hand in friendship, and glad I am for the chance.

THE FIELD

Wild birds and bent flowers in the weed-sotted, sapling-sown, straw-stubbled field. I drive by on crowded Route 235. Notice how it yawns in the midst of concrete and brick: flutter of peace, sigh of silence, one breath, one blink, it's gone.

Or not. It must exist somewhere inside me, because later in the day I can summon it. Flutter, sigh, breath, blink. Amidst thoughts hard as concrete, worries dense as brick, behold: an empty field. Space for wild birds and bent flowers in a crowded mind.

Now I look to make tryst with it, like any eager lover. Some mornings, a thick mist hovers tenderly just above the broken chaff. Some afternoons, shafts of sunlight turn tufts of grass into emeralds. At night, while I'm sleeping, my field remains awake. To embrace whatever errant moonbeams or wandering starshine might be lurking about. All these my field can hold – the mist, the light, the moon, the stars – because it's empty.

Consider the atom. Its nucleus – protons and neutrons – is 100,000 times smaller than the cloud of orbiting electrons that surrounds it. If the atom were a cathedral, its nucleus would be a speck of dust. The atom is mostly empty.

You and I, the moon and the stars, the birds, the flowers – we're all composed of atoms. We are all mostly empty space, no more solid than chicken wire, which derives its strength from structure, not from mass. Positively charged protons, attracting negatively charged electrons, that's what we're made of: electromagnetic currents circulating in a vacant field.

You think you're sitting on a chair? You're actually hovering 10 to the minus 8 centimeters over it, the electrons of your body repelling the electrons of the chair. Substance is an illusion. In-

Invisible forces of attraction and repulsion arrange our world into visible patterns, and these forces need free and open space in which to operate. Emptiness is what holds everything together. Nothingness makes all somethings possible.

Now we've come to the season of merry and sparkle and flash. Of buy and give and do and go filling every nook and cranny of every day and every night. If December were an atom, it would collapse in on itself, puddle into nothingness because of too much something. Just the opposite of the season's religious symbols. Hanukkah: a purified temple newly open to receive worshipers. Christmas: an empty manger waiting for a newborn babe.

And what about us? My field is slated for development, soon to be filled with more of the same, the same, the same. No room at that inn anymore, no space for flutter or sigh, no echo to the silent, holy nothingness that makes possible all our somethings. Where will they play, the invisible forces that give rise to our visible patterns, to moonbeams and starshine and people who open empty arms to embrace each other?

Unless we find a way – Find a way! – to keep some fields free for wild birds and bent flowers and you and me.

▣ ▣ ▣

CATCHING THE LIGHT

Blue skies and brittle cold at Myrtle Point that day. Threading my way past twisted stalks of sea oats, with the stubble of marsh grass underfoot, and the small surf cascading along the beach in falling dominos of sound. Mesmerized by the sparkling strokes of sun's pen crosshatched on water's crumpled surface. Dazed by a shimmering ribbon of wet sand curled along the shoreline. Glimmering motes of seedstuff in the air. Glinting insect wings. Flashing filaments of spidersilk anchored to the bushes, floating in the breeze, invisible except in this one shining moment, when, just so, they catch the light.

Then I saw them, freshly minted by the ebbing tide. I picked up one, then another: glistening pebbles like frosted glass. I couldn't fathom why, but I had to have more, so I ran that day up and down the beach, rejecting anything solidly white, plucking up anything translucent, stuffing my coat pockets, hurrying home with my treasures, and it's only as I write that understanding dawns: carbonic acid in the water has leeched away their salts. Once opaque, these stones have offered their very substance to the river. Now they are transparent bearers of the light.

But the days grow darker. Light is ebbing, like the tide. One of my stones is oval, another, round. Earth's axis of rotation is 23.5° off vertical. As she treads her elliptical path around the sun, she points first her northern then her southern hemisphere toward it. Starting June 21st, the sun loses altitude in our noontime sky, and this inexorable progression of shortening days and lengthening nights climaxes on December 21st, the winter solstice, the 'sun still' day, when our star halts its southbound journey and turns north once more so that light, like the tide, can flow forth again.

Ignorant of Earth's tilt and the science of rotation, our ancestors were frightened this time of year. What if the sun keeps going? What if it never comes back? Rituals evolved to catch it, hold it, convince it to return, celebrate when it did. Today we know the sun will reverse its pendulum swing without our help, yet the Hanukkah menorah, the Scandinavian Yule log, the candles of the Christmas tree or Kwanzaa kinara: all our festivals during this season are efforts to push back the cold and dark with warmth and light. One of my personal rituals is an evening drive through the countryside to look at all the houses. So bold, those sparkles and shimmers. So brave, those glimmers and glints. So defiant, all that shining, when night presses close around and threatens to snuff it out.

This Christmas morning it will be fifty years since my father died, so I know something about the dimming. As do we all. Earth rotates daily at 1,000 miles an hour, revolves yearly at 67,000 miles an hour. Amidst all this spinning and tilting the losses keep coming, the griefs pile up, and what are we in an ocean of trouble but small stones scraping in an ineluctable tide? Rejoice, I say, and rejoice again, because in this briny swash and backwash our opaque substance wears away, making us, with every day that passes, more translucent.

Einstein himself said light is a mystery. It is pure energy interfacing with matter at its electrical and magnetic levels. The sun is our primary light source, but the arena of interaction which scientists call electromagnetic radiation occurs in and around all objects, including you and me. What if we go one step further than Einstein, and use another word for light: love. Isn't that pure energy? Doesn't love interface with matter at, shall we say, the highest level? So rejoice, I say, and rejoice again, because the tiniest act of kindness is a radiant force, invisible except in the one shining moment when, just so, we catch the light.

THE FULCRUM

Depending on the moment in humanity's evolutionary history at which you choose to begin counting – cranium size? walking upright? use of tools? – our species is 2 to 3.7 million years old. The holidays on which most of us lavish our celebratory energies in December – Kwanzaa, Christmas, New Year's, Hanukkah – have been around for 43, for 1,673, for 2,162 and for 2,174 years, respectively. Not only are they extremely new, these feasts, they are also divisive, a continual reminder of heritages, the naming of which forces us to see ourselves as similar to some but different than most other human beings.

What about celebrating something we all share? Something that aligns us with mystery, and with those forces at work throughout the universe that have guided and energized humanity for all of its several million year history. What about that big fiery ball up in the sky? The one that gives us, you know, everything? Dawn, dusk, light, life, energy, you name it, the sun provides it, and on the 21st of December it does the most amazing, stupendous, monumentally meaningful thing on the planet: it stops its apparent southward journey, stands still in the sky, then turns north again so that our short, shorter, shortest days begin to reclaim their long, longer, longest status.

The writer John Fowles says, "There comes a time in each life like a point of fulcrum. At that time you must accept yourself. It is not anymore what you will become. It is what you are and always will be." December 21st is nature's fulcrum, the pivot about which the lever of our days and nights revolves. I'm wondering if the 21st Century could be humanity's fulcrum, the moment in evolutionary history when we accept a fact that has grown short, shorter, shortest in our consciousness; that is, we will never become greater than the web of life through, with and in which we were fashioned. We are and always will be part of a single sacred community called Earth (long), called the Milky Way (longer), called the Universe (longest), and this, it seems to me, is something we can all raise a glass to this season.

No need to shelve our Santas, our crèches, our dreidels, our Swahili dictionaries in order to reclaim our large, larger, largest status. Just look up into the sky on December 21st and say to the sun, "We are no longer diminishing, you and I, we have changed direction, and henceforth, we shall be increasing."

BLUE MOON

It hung in the sky from sunset to sunrise, spanning the last day of 2009 and the first day of 2010. A quixotic event that, every two to three years, arrives now in one season, now in another, bestowing upon the month of its appearance a second full moon which, because it is outside all systems of lunar nomenclature, has no proper name and is called, simply, blue. On December 2, 2009 we had an oak, cold or long night moon, while on December 31, 2009, we had a blue moon which, as I've already pointed out, shone its uncommon light on the last hours of 2009 and the first hours of 2010, becoming, as it were, a bridge. A yoke. A hinge. Making, of the two distinct years, one indivisible unit.

Leaping from astronomy to quantum physics, I'd like to point out something else. Scientists can demonstrate in their labs that, while atoms are mostly empty, the emptiness is not really a void but, rather, a cloud of possibility out of which protons, neutrons and electrons appear and disappear. Matter isn't solid at all, it's a furling unfurling abyss from which substance manifests, and, according to Superstring Theory, the newest scientific model, all those particles as well as the gravity that binds them together form, not separate objects or distinct forces, but an indivisible strand of energy in constant communication with itself.

Leaping from quantum physics to a recent walk on the beach, I'd like to tell you about the dead heron I found. I felt compelled to spread out its wings, as if the bird were still flying. To stretch out its neck, as if it were heading westward. To place, in its beak, the dead fish lying next to it. Then I scrubbed my hands with sand, rinsed them in waves that flapped on the beach like wings, continued my stroll. Later, going back to my car, I heard a rifle's report in the woods.

And realized: that heron had been shot from the sky in full flight, its dinner wriggling in its mouth.

Where did it come from, the impulse to re-enact the heron's last few minutes of life? I believe there was a silent tug on the strand of energy linking our bodies. You can believe what you want, but let me point out that the first year of the second decade of the only new millennium any of us will ever know has begun in exceptional fashion, linked by a rare and special light to the year preceding it, asking us to pay attention to that which is bridged, yoked, hinged together. It is not a concatenation of separate objects, this universe we inhabit, it is a continuum, an indivisible unit existing for a common purpose, unto a common promise. What is it they say? "United we stand, divided we fall." Patrick Henry and Mahatma Gandhi used it of their separate nations, perhaps this year we'll learn to use it of the continuum called Earth.

THE JOURNEY

When the sun sets. When the sun sets on my river. When the sun sets on my river, and the wings of gulls turn to white gold. And the leaves of trees turn to green gold. And the clouds turn into carnelian cobblestones that pave, east to west across trembling waters, a red gold road. Then, yes, I shall find me some shoes of gold vermillion. And a sturdy gilded staff. I shall set my feet upon this crimson highway, and before too long I shall meet the evening star.

When the sun rises. When the sun rises on my river. When the sun rises on my river, and an incoming tide of light submerges, one by one, the sky's small pebbles of light. And the leaves of trees emerge from silhouette. And the groaning onyx waters turn to flashing silver sighs. Then, yes, I shall know I have arrived, face to face with the morning star.

And yes, I think it matters, that my celestial assignation is not with a star at all but with a planet. Venus. Except for the moon, Venus is the brightest object in our sky, in closer orbit to the sun than Earth. First to appear in the gloaming, last to disappear at dawn. Alpha and omega. Venus, the planet named for love and beauty, who watches over our endings and beginnings.

In Roman times, the goddess appeared in many guises. Venus *Cloacina*, the Purifier, giver of peace. Venus *Genetrix*, the great Mother, who bestowed fertility on folk and field. Venus *Felix*, the Lucky; *Amica*, the Friend; *Libertina*, the Free; *Obsequens*, the Graceful; and, *Verticordia*, the Changer of Hearts. Venus. Our morning and evening star. Fashioned from the same nebula that formed the planet Earth, named for all our yearnings, watching over.

The sun has set on the river of time we called 'last year.' Rises now on the same river, called 'this year.' Pause. When you set out along this highway, where were you going? Are you sure you want to arrive there? Take stock. Is there something you might wish to put down? Something else more suited to this journey you think you might wish to take up?

Get serious. It matters. All the fields and all the folk, all the planets and the stars, we're all made from the same stuff. Protons, neutrons, electrons. A trembling flow of atoms and molecules. Action and reaction. Electromagnetic currents that groan and sigh. One vast and mighty river, what happens to me happens to you happens to them and it forever.

Ask questions. The year is just beginning. You have 365 days, 8,760 hours, 525,600 minutes until it ends. Let's say today is the morning star, still lingering in the dawn of last year. Before she appears as evening star in the year's gloaming, what do you want to accomplish? Think. Don't answer off the top of your head. Don't answer for yourself alone. Look beyond family, neighborhood, country. Look beyond your own lifetime. One vast and mighty river, remember?

What happens to me happens to you happens to them and it forever.

And don't be glib. Don't say "world peace" if you don't mean "world peace." If you're not ready to do something to make this a more peaceful world. And if you're not ready, admit it. Spend the year asking the Changer of Hearts to change yours. I'll do the same. What happens to me happens to you happens to them and it forever.

So when the sun sets on our river of minutes, hours, days, years. When the flow of atoms ceases for you and me. We shall leave behind our trembling and our sighs, and ready ourselves to set out upon a golden highway. To meet, face to face, that from which we were fashioned. Our alpha and our omega, the sum of all our yearnings. When the sun rises.

NOTES OF A NATIVE DAUGHTER*

Often, in the journal that is my heart, the only entry is a note about how the sun looked on the Chesapeake Bay that day. If it sparkled. If it spread across the surface like a sheet of silver silk. If it disappeared altogether into heavy leaden swells.

Other days are more eventful. Everything that's ever happened to me is there, in the journal that is my heart, even the things I would like to erase because they cause more hurt than I want to endure, or because they fill me with a sharp and bitter anger, or because they prove I am not nearly as good a person as I'd like to believe myself to be and hence, make me ashamed.

* Author's note. This was published on January 21, 2009.

Last year I discovered something that warranted a long entry in my journal. The Chesapeake Bay has a hole in it. Some 35 million years ago, a giant meteorite crashed to Earth, gouging a deep crater in the ocean floor. Millions of tons of water, sediment and shattered rock spewed into the air for hundreds of miles along the east coast, and the resulting tsunami may have overtopped the Blue Ridge Mountains.

The hole has filled in over the eons, of course. Until 1983, no one even suspected its existence, because the crater – twice the size of Rhode Island and nearly as deep as the Grand Canyon – is buried 300 to 500 meters beneath the lower bay and its surrounding peninsulas. Acknowledged or not, the chasm makes its presence felt. Continual slumping of rubble within it affects the course of rivers. Groundwater is easily contaminated by subsurface salt. All four major earthquakes in the region were near or inside the trace of the crater rim.

Last year I made another long entry in the journal that is my heart. An African American was elected president of the United States. He was inaugurated yesterday, on January 20th, the day after we celebrated the birthday of another African American whose dream has been inscribed in the journal that is the American heart.

I've been re-reading Martin Luther King's touchstone speech. I've also been re-reading James Baldwin's *Notes of a Native Son*. And I've been thinking about that hole underneath the Chesapeake Bay. After the meteor struck, the sea floor around the crater became a dead zone for some 3,000 years. King and Baldwin both describe the dead zone created by slavery: segregation, discrimination, oppression, injustice. The burden of shame shouldered by generation after generation of white Americans. The loneliness endured by generation after generation of black Americans, exiles in their own land. Everyone scrabbling for so long in the hard soil of mutual fear.

These things are penned in the journals of all our hearts, we cannot erase them, but we can turn the page now and start something new. I have on my desk an announcement from the

Calvert Gazette, dated June 21, 1919. It says that "the colored voters of Calvert County" have taken stock of "the very valuable part they had taken in the war" and think themselves "entitled to some political recognition." Consequently, "they decided to endeavor to put a colored man on the ticket this fall." Political recognition of value and entitlement. An affirmation of equality. This inauguration is that, and more. It is, if you will, proof that life has been restored after a devastating impact event.

America will always be affected by her slave-owning past, just as she will always be shaped by the destruction of her indigenous culture. Forever we will be subject to slumpings of a particular kind of rubble, to unique subsurface tensions, to fault lines that invite inexorable seismic disturbances, these are our collective heritage. But something else is ours as well, yes? Something we've inherited as a people? It is the capacity to transform our weaknesses into strengths.

Martin Luther King prophesied that one day we would "hew out of the mountain of despair a stone of hope." Barack Obama insisted, "Yes, we can." Whatever shape the stone of hope takes, I am glad I'm one of 300 million Americans carving it.

SHADOWS

Don't read this. You'll end up like me, falling Alice-fashion through a rabbit hole into a topsy-turvy world. You'll never be the same again, if you manage to escape, which you may not manage at all.

Still here? Well, I warned you, so, okay, I was driving south on Route 235. All that flat, black, boring macadam. Those tedious, humdrum stores. I was minding my own business, you understand, neither wishing for this nor hoping for that, not expecting anything except more of what I already had when I saw a scroll-work, a filigree, a lacy marvel of delicate shapes splashed and spangled across the road. Shadows. Cast by the 3 o'clock sun beaming behind a strip of skinny, skimpy, barren trees growing forlornly along the curb.

That was the hole, and I fell hard. Flagpoles, traffic lights, cars, garbage cans ... stripped of their detail and pared down to pure outline, they all possessed an exotic and intoxicating beauty. Mesmerized, I could hardly drive myself home, but even there I was no longer safe. My same-old, same-old venetian blinds turned a blank wall into a spectacular gridwork of slanting lines. An unremarkable collection of objects atop my coffee table changed a bland carpet into a fantasy garden.

What did I tell you? See? Now you're stuck, same as me, scoping out the nooks and crannies of your formerly ho-hum existence. Have you noticed? Depending on the angle of the light source, shadows faithfully mimic but hopelessly distort their originals. Thicker, thinner, longer, shorter, awry, askew, tilted. Objects get duplicated every which-a-way on any which-a-thing: a mailbox on a barn roof, a person climbing a chimney, why, just this morning a tree grew itself right through my window and onto my dining table, bringing a soft breeze with it on trembling leaves.

Shadows are the funhouse surprise hidden in life's serious underbelly, but they can have important consequences. Peter Pan risked everything to get his back, and its recovery inaugurated the journey to NeverNever Land. Where would we be without Tinker Bell and Captain Hook? Then there's that pesky groundhog, whose amblings make no sense at all, I mean, if the creature sees his shadow, the sun's out and spring should be closer, not further away, but the folks up in Punxsutawney, Pennsylvania have invented some flabberdiflap about a Candelemas Day legend, which you can check out for yourself, I don't give it much credence.

A rain shadow is a dry area behind a mountain range. Sound vanishes into an acoustic shadow. The psychologist Carl Jung called the negative parts of ourselves we don't want to admit we have our shadow. He said real maturity only comes when we take responsibility for those ugly, unwelcome newsflashes from the soul's frontier. It's still winter, but when I walked through the woods last week all the multiflora vines sported bright new leaves. Is that a shadow? I don't know, Alice, it's just you and me together in this topsy-turvy world.

⊡ ⊡ ⊡

EVERYTHING CURVES

Crimson, his dog was called. His name, I didn't catch, distracted as I was by the reverberating shapes: snaking shoreline; great rippled swags of water sweeping the beach, crimping the sand; undulating heaps of seaweed at the wrack line; crescent-shaped shells; the flight of gulls spiraling over the horizon's arc. It was cold. Hoods drawn tight against the wind, we stopped to chat, our distinct trajectories of interest (his, collecting driftwood; mine, notes for a poem) bending into each other, briefly, then arcing away, although I can still see the worm eaten shard of log he held in his hand: circular holes bored by soft, round bodies on their serpentine journey through the wood.

Everything curves, it seems. The rounded breast of the robin, the oak tree's bushy green orb, even the space-time fabric, with its warp threads of length, height, depth and its weft threads of duration. Gravity itself is not a force of attraction but a curvature, the shape an interaction takes when a heavier object (our sun, for instance, or a bowling ball on your bedspread) creates a circular depression in space around which a lighter object (Earth, for instance, or a marble on your bed) travels, despite whatever trajectory it might have assumed prior to this encounter. How this affects the stream of minutes and hours I don't entirely understand, but I do know that, when I'm with my lover, time seems to slow down, to stop entirely, to speed up, then cease, utterly, to matter, for why trouble oneself over a measuring tool so erratic, so unreliable? Better to rejoice in the wild and gleeful spin, the unexpected shape one life takes when circling around another.

In the year 270, the Roman Emperor Claudius II decided that unattached males made better soldiers than those with families, so he outlawed marriage for young men. St. Valentine defied the emperor by performing such weddings in secret, and when Claudius found out, he threw the priest in prison where, according to legend, he fell in love with his jailor's daughter. The night before his execution, he wrote the girl a letter, which he signed, "From your Valentine." Both courageous and romantic, Valentine became one of the church's most revered saints, and Pope Gelasius I declared February 14th his feast day in the year 498, probably in an attempt to Christianize the pagan fertility feast, Lupercalia, the celebration of which included a large urn from which Roman bachelors drew the names of the young women with whom they would pair for the upcoming year.

Everything curves, it seems. Some priest spirals around the need of young couples to be married. Some jailor's daughter spins around him. The story grows heavier over the years, bending the space-time fabric, creating an ever-larger vortex into which more couples slip, slide, spin. Minutes and hours speed up, slow down, cease, utterly, to matter. Life trajectories change shape. The serpentine journey is rearranged. Hearts twine into each other, as on a crimson card signed, “From your Valentine.”

CLOUDS

The language they use is not my language, nor is my horizon theirs. That much I know. And I know, too, that at any given moment, 10 thousand stories with 60 thousand possible endings float in my head, clouds on the wind of thought but if I. Just. Look. Up. I can be part of a shape shifting epic far beyond my paltry efforts to imagine or control.

What gets me about clouds is how every one is an absolutely unique and unrepeatable variation on an absolutely constant theme. As water evaporates from Earth's surface, the molecules latch onto dust particles floating in the air Warm air holds more water vapor than cool air, so when those two meet – over, say, a mountain or an ocean – the excess vapor condenses into minute droplets. Or, if it's very cold – above 20,000 feet – into ice crystals. Clouds are visible accumulations of these invisible condensations, floating in our lower atmosphere, drifting with the wind. From space, clouds look like a tattered cloak hugging the blue shoulders of our planet. From Earth, clouds look. Anyway. They. Can.

Smears, globs, puffs, clumps, up, down, in-between. High thin veil, low thick blanket. A shred far away, a wisp close by. Floating apart, joining together. Sometimes tranquil, sometimes furious. So many outside factors can influence a cloud. Wind, light, temperature. So much is going on inside a cloud. Tiny droplets get warmer, bigger, maybe heavy enough to overcome an updraft, fall as rain, maybe not. The droplets combine, leave larger spaces between. Less light reflects, more absorbs, hence, those sunbright tops and shadowdark bottoms, that amazing range of seething whites and eddying grays, roiled by dawn or sunset to red, orange, pink, purple. A swirling, surging, pulsing aliveness.

Yes, that's it. Clouds are alive, the same as you and I. I know myself as I was up until this moment, but I don't know myself as I could be tomorrow. I'm all possibility, perpetually changing within, continually responding to changes without. Forces, factors, circumstances, people. A mutable 'me' in a shifting 'we.' Floating apart, joining together. An absolutely unique and unrepeatable variation on an absolutely constant theme.

I think we'd be lonely without them, don't you? Especially in winter, clouds are ephemeral companions, assuaging the emptiness of a vast and relentless sky. They add texture and depth and beauty to an otherwise flat and boring plane. Some people like to categorize them. *Cumulus* for 'heap,' *stratus* for 'layer,' a prefix of 'alto' or 'cirr' to designate height. Some people like to name them, populating the void above with a comforting array of familiar shapes: rabbits or birds or ice cream cones. Me, I'd rather abandon my own agenda and just watch. An alphabet of white and gray. A grammar of motion and rest. An exotic language of limitless horizons spelling out heroic tales of unbounded potential I can always aspire to, hope for. Available to all of us, ev-

ery day, without effort or cost, if we would only.

Look. Up.

◘ ◘ ◘

CARDINALS

A flick, a flash, a fizz. Dash of, startle of, zing of red. The cardinal. Color of my beating heart, pumping blood. Color of the flame that brightens my dark, cooks my food, warms my cold. Red. For good luck in China, purity in India, courage in Europe, joy in Russia, mourning in South Africa, success among the Cherokee, death for the Celts. Red. Stimulates brain waves, quickens respiration, raises blood pressure. Symbolizes danger, energy, passion, power, anger, desire. Used in brothels, on fire trucks, stop signs and as a bouquet to signify undying love.

Small wonder, then, that this little crimson chit is a state bird seven times over. Illinois, Indiana, Kentucky, North Carolina, Ohio, Virginia and West Virginia have all claimed the cardinal as their own, and I must confess, I've been smitten, too. My lips just can't help it; they need to stretch from ear to ear as soon as my eyes register his allegro arrival on branch or feeder. I love the way he's sharp all over: pointy crest, razor-edged whistle; quick, keen snaps of tail and head. Never still, this bird, never dull. Always a spark of bright and cheer, especially in winter.

In the 1800's, cardinals were confined to the American southeast. Prized for their color and song, they were trapped and sold as cage birds to European markets, a lively trade that terminated with the Migratory Bird Treaty of 1918. As human settlement changed dense forests into bushes and parks, the bird's range expanded, and now, wherever the annual precipitation tops 16 inches, he zips around on a feathered wavelength of 750 nanometers.

Cardinals are helpful. They eat weed seeds and harmful insects, including the voracious seventeen-year locust. Both sexes cooperate equally in child-rearing, not unusual in the avian world, but what is unique to the species is the way males and females share song phrases, stitching together their separate patches to make one melodious quilt. Not a bad model. Cooperation leads to peace, peace leads to joy, who knows where joy might lead.

I looked it up in the dictionary. It means "a vivid emotion of pleasure arising from a sense of well-being." The root word is *joie*, jewel. A joyous spirit sparkles, a glad heart shines, a ruby-red bird flashes forth what's hidden in the secret heart of the world. Season by season. A stun of scarlet on snow. A surprise of crimson on budding branch, in dense foliage. A fat feathered berry at harvest time.

So I have a plan. The cardinal will be my decimal point for happiness, my bookmark for gladness. Every time I smile to see one I'll remember to rush right out and share a song with someone, or beat back some weeds, or vote for universal health care, or put an end to war, I don't know, all it has to do is make someone feel a little better, a little safer, then, flick, flash, fizz, there's a dash more joy in the world.

WE SHALL BE CHANGED

The gulls cartwheel in ever-widening spirals, their cries scraping the air like rusty hinges. "Fly away," I think, admonishing them. "The river's over there; you don't belong in the WalMart parking lot." But the gulls pay no attention to me, just as, in New Mexico, the ravens in parking lots failed to respond to my telepathic chiding. "Must you parade yourselves on this ugly asphalt," I told them, "with such beautiful mesas everywhere around?"

It's the pot calling the kettle black, I suppose. There was a small country store up on one of those mesas, close to where I lived, yet I drove 30 miles to stock my shelves from Walmart's more ample supplies. And today? By driving a few miles out of my way to shop on Solomon's Island, I could have crossed the bridge and treated myself to a glimmer of infinity sparkling up and down the Patuxent River. Yet here I am with the gulls at Walmart, practical and pragmatic.

The other night, I was warming up before an exercise class. I overheard a woman next to me say to someone else, "You know that new shopping center? They're going to open a Kohl's." There was reverence in her voice as she uttered the department store's name, and her joyful anticipation was echoed by another woman, who piped in, excitedly, "There's going to be an Olive Garden."

Their obvious and passionate longing shocked me, because just a few hours earlier I'd been at the beach. The chalky white arc of a quarter moon swam in a cold blue sky, its shape echoed by the curved breast of a swan floating on blue water, echoed again by crescent-shaped clam shells, bleached white and littering the iron-hard sand. At the wrack line, the perpetual ebb and unceasing flow of swash and backwash had etched themselves onto an old tree stump, sculpting solid wood into fluid, rippled slivers.

Earth, sea and sky seemed to meet in that moment, their boundaries softened as they offered themselves each to each to be reshaped, refashioned, changed.

People need food, shelter and clothing. But once we have the basics, do we then need more food, bigger shelters, fancier clothes? What about the wonder needed by human intelligence, the beauty needed by human imagination, the intimacy with mystery needed by the human spirit? Contact with the natural world assuages our thirst for the divine. Can brand-name stores or restaurants make the same claim? When all the land is gone, will we be happy offering ourselves up to the transforming action of asphalt?

So these gulls and I, we're leaving this place. We're going back to the beach, where we belong. We shall stand at the wrack line, where earth and sea and sky meet, and we shall remember that spring – with its rebirth of wonder, beauty and mystery – is not so far away. We shall notice there's a glimmer of infinity sparkling up and down the river, and we shall surrender ourselves to it. We shall be changed.

KEEPER OF THE LIGHT

Closely manicured by swift salt winds, cedars huddle near the lighthouse at Piney Point, Maryland. I stand on the pier staring down at the Potomac, where swift salt currents rush in and out simultaneously. The schizophrenic tide creates tense ripples on the river's surface, treacherous eddies in its depths, and just now seems to be influencing a flock of swallows, which zig and zag crazily in staggered, frantic flight.

I have no clue what might have drawn me here today, just that I've been thinking about lighthouses for some time now, ever since I read a series of journal entries describing the 1633 Atlantic crossing of one of Maryland's founding fathers. Furious winds, fearsome pirates, boisterous seas, smashed rudders. A ship that drifts "like a dish in the water, at the mercy of the waves." Sure, and anyone who picks up a newspaper these days will find echoes of that harrowing account.

I think I would have enjoyed my job, had I been keeper of the light here. I imagine gadding about during the day, collecting oyster shells in colors to match my moods: white for happy, gray for sad, ochre-stained for pensive times, lavender-tinted when contentment rules. The crimson flag of the setting sun alerts me to hurry home, where I transfer all my treasures to some shelf, careful to leave there with them my vagrant feelings.

All night I keep vigil with beacon or foghorn, as the weather requires, but my duty goes beyond flipping some switch. I picture them in my mind, men and women in their fragile boats, storm-tossed, afraid for their lives, their cries woven into the fabric of swift salt winds. They need whatever light I can give them, shining forth from the nearby tower, or shining forth from that smaller observatory, my heart.

I remember reading something in the *Washington Post* a few months back, about how happiness can spread among people rather like a virus. Studies show our emotional state depends as much on others' choices, actions and experiences as it does on our own, and the statistics are counter-intuitive. A joyful next-door neighbor, whom I may not know well, can increase my joy factor by 34%, while a spouse's happiness will only bolster mine by 8%. This inverse correlation between intimacy and impact leads to some interesting speculations. It suggests, for instance, that in troubled times like these, I have a responsibility to keep watch over my own vagrant emotions, especially fear. I must keep my heart's lens clear, as it were, so that whatever light I possess – faith, hope, love – will continuc to radiate out invisibly but brightly, reaching those endangered by despair's boisterous seas. And what if, by some small kindness, I can make just one stranger happy? Then the domino effect kicks in, and that person's entire network will get a jolt of joy.

Today's paper may bring news of schizophrenic tides, tense ripples, treacherous eddies, but I am the keeper of the light, and I have a job to do.

A DIFFERENT KIND OF WONDERFUL

Low tide when I was there this morning. The virgin sand smooth and gleaming, like a waxed wood floor. A heron, way down the beach. Long legs planted in the shallow surf. Long neck curling into her breast, making a tight "S," uncurling, making a tilted "C." An "S" and a "C," the first two letters of her call. "Scrank, scrank," she cries, harsh and throaty, when she takes flight.

So I'm doing my usual thing, collecting any object that grabs my attention for reasons that, crystal clear in the moment of reaching, become confused in the moment of possession. "Why *this*," I ask myself, staring at the umpteenth mussel shell I've plucked up in the last half hour.

They're all identical: a luminescent splash of violet and indigo on the inside. Drab black or brown on the outside, mottled with white. Some are as long as my finger, others smaller than the nail on my pinky. I keep at it, my self-appointed task, eagerly snatching up every shell I find, then wondering what the urgency is all about.

So I'm doing that, my usual thing, when I see these three gashes in the sand. Like a trident, with the middle prong taller and deeper than those flanking it. One set, then another beside that, then two others ahead of those, and I realize, these gouges were made by a heron's sharp talons. I follow in her steps, placing each of my feet just so, next to hers, but then the tracks abruptly cease. "Scrank, scrank," she must have cried just there, harsh and throaty, and I pluck up the solitary, bluegray feather she left for me, as if pitying my inability to trail her into the luminescent air.

Now I'm back home, doing my usual thing, emptying pockets and bags. While putting all the mussel shells together in a bowl, I see that what I'd thought were white splotches are actually a mother-of-pearl lining peeking through. And that every bi-valve shell curves left or right. I sort them by size, reuniting the companion pairs, which fit just so, side by side, like wings, and I place the bowl just so, next to the seed pods I found last week, also companion pairs, a top and a bottom, but these aren't wings, they're little boats. Some curve starboard, some curve to port. Their deep, narrow hulls taper to a sharp tip at the bow and flatten out at the stern.

So I did my usual thing. Obeyed my heart, not my head. By letting the blind promptings of one moment's reaching carry me beyond confusion, I've arrived at a moment of pure and emergent wonder. And now I have a choice to make, what do you think? Should I hop in my boat and sail away? Or should I slip into my wings and, scrank, scrank, disappear, leaving you with a choice to make, too. Stay where you are? Or follow me into the luminescent air?

Rock Chorus

Today they are submerged by the tide, their voices muffled. Two swans swim above them, foraging. Listening? A solitary heron stands in the shallow breakwater, the blue-gray smudge of his folded wings echoed by the blue-gray storm clouds unfurling overhead. He does not fool me, this heron, with his fisherman's vigilant pretense, I know he has come here to eavesdrop, same as I.

I heard them last month for the first time. A winter storm's swirling skirts had chased the Chesapeake's waters out to sea. The rocks lay glistening in the sloping sand as if standing on risers. I knew they were singing the same way a hummingbird knows a flower holds nectar: by its own body's instinctive hovering.

I hovered. My beak opened to imbibe. All colors, shapes, textures, sizes. Each its own impenetrable and inviolate self, yet each a fragment of some lost whole, a cipher for the eons. Some may have traveled here frozen in the ice of an ancient glacier. Others could have been spewed from a volcano now extinct and crumbled to dust. Still others might once have been clods of dirt in Jurassic gardens where primeval flowers bloomed. Call them rocks, or call them musical notes: earth, air, water, fire. Composed by pressure, arranged by accident, and by time.

The sun was bright that day. I picked up one large stone and held it aloft. Shades of ox-blood, ocher, umber, shot through with black flecks, gray striations. The wet surface sparkled in the light, and a phrase from that biblical collection of love poems, the *Song of Songs*, shot through my head. "Set me like a seal on your heart," I heard the rock sing, "Like a shield on your arm. For love is stronger than death, vast flames cannot quench it nor rivers sweep it away." I put the stone back down among its fellow choristers, and smiled, and walked away.

In today's leaden light, the metallic waters of the Bay swell sullenly. The economy, along with other critical components of life on this planet, seems to be collapsing, and we can only hope our leaders are capable of steering us through this crisis. Crisis. From the ancient Greek, *krino*, meaning, 'to choose, to judge, to decide.'

I am just a little clod of dirt. Some of my molecules were frozen in the ice of an ancient glacier. Others spewed from a volcano now extinct. Tonight I will go outside and look up at the stars, stacked in the night sky like rocks on a beach. I'll listen to the throbbing pulse of crickets, and I'll sing with them, for vast flames cannot quench love, nor can rivers sweep it away. And if by chance you should be eavesdropping on us, by all means, feel free to join the lithic chorus, because whatever decisions we make, we are making together, fragments of a lost whole, ciphers for the eons.

⊡ ⊡ ⊡

STILL NIGHT, TWIN MOONS

Sun and wind have disappeared this night, and it is still. I recognize nothing and yet I know everything, especially this wintry moon. This silver disk that leaves me almost aghast at such perfect roundness, almost appalled at such perfect brilliance, almost confused because tonight there are two moons. One above, one below. One in the cloudless sky, one in the motionless water. In fact, as I look around I see that everything is doubled this night. The uneven silhouette of the treeline, a little white shed on the opposite shore, a boat moored at my neighbor's dock, all are twinned in the river's glassy surface.

A palindrome is a sequence of units that reads the same forward or back. Words like "radar" and "noon." Phrases such as "Damn mad!" Numbers, for example, "16461" or "12/02/2021." Even DNA – those spiraled threads that teach all life how to grow – even the nucleotides of our genetic coding can mirror each other. A recent genome sequencing project discovered that a palindromic structure allows the Y chromosome to repair itself by bending over at the middle so that a healthy twin can replace its damaged counterpart.

Which brings me to the dark, still night that some call contemplative prayer. "For you alone my soul in silence waits." For a long time I used this line when I prayed, sometimes repeating it like a mantra, sometimes settling into the silence and just letting the phrase arise when it would. The sentence paraphrases Psalm 130, and I can't remember where I picked it up – a set of taped chants, perhaps? I've been praying it off and on for 20 years now, always as an expression of *my* silent waiting, always directed to a 'you' who is God. But just the other day it came to me, in a quiet, eureka moment: the 'you' is 'me' and the one waiting in silence for me is God. We are all palindromes. Our divine twin forever bends over us, repairing the damage to our true nature, but in the mesmerizing sights and sounds of daytime, how can we arrive at such deep knowing? Contemplative prayer is the windless, moonlit evening that allows me to say, as Catherine of Genoa said 500 years ago, "My me is God, nor do I recognize any other me except my God."

Which brings me back to this moment, sitting here on this pier. The curling shore is silver-gilt, a lavish frame, and the river is fastened to earth, mirror to wall. Making a mirror is a painstaking process involving so many grains of Silver Nitrate and Rochelle Salts, so many pints of distilled water and ammonia, much stirring and dissolving, straining and filtering. The glass must be warm, and absolutely clean, for the least speck of dust or grease will show in the backing and mar the reflection on the finished surface. Isn't that what life is? A painstaking process involving so many grains of struggle, so many pints of hurt, a stirring of joy, filtering of mistakes, the warmth of love and we become God-mirrors. "Now we

see as in a reflection," says Paul of Tarsus. "Then

we shall know clearly, even as we are known." But do we have to wait until some distant future? Can't we be who we really are today?

Like many another in this newest and most fragile of centuries, I am plagued by anxiety. There's a line in scripture, in Peter's first letter: "Your opponent the devil is prowling like a roaring lion, looking for someone to devour." My anxiety seemed just such a ravenous beast, I struggled with it constantly, until I borrowed a peacemaker's tip from the Buddhist teacher Thich Nhat Hahn: treat the offending feeling like a suffering child, not an enemy. Envelop it with compassion, not hate. Then memory turned up a very different passage, from Isaiah: "The wolf will lie down with the lamb, the calf with the lion will feed. There shall be no harm or hurt on all my holy mountain, for the earth is filled with the knowledge of God as water swells the sea." Yet we seem to resist this knowing, clinging to our conflicts, inner and outer, afraid to recognize ourselves, aghast, appalled, at our true brilliance.

A stone's throw from this dock, a solitary piling stands erect in the tranquil, moon-bright water. It's impossible to tell where post ends and reflection begins. Be still. Be still and know. Be still and know that I am God, says the psalm, says the wooden post, the white shed, the motionless trees. If ever I wanted a book that would tell me what peace really means, that book is here: peace means not knowing where God ends and we begin.

DECIPHERING THE SEASON

Paleography. From the Greek. *Paleos*, old, *graphos*, written. The work of the palaeographer is to decipher the writings of the past. Fascinated by the relationship between the human hand and the text it generated, medieval practitioners of this budding science studied the *ductos*: the movement of the pen while forming letters. They also learned abbreviations, punctuation, ligatures – all in an effort to understand a scribe's style, so they could assign to the writing a date and place of origin.

Today's practitioner – that would be me – is equally fascinated by the *ductos* that confronts her now: the hand of nature forming letters on this beach. Date and place of origin is no mys-

tery: early March. The Chesapeake Bay. But I think there is a message here. I think someone is trying to tell me something. I think I would be – what? Happier? Wiser? More complete? The stakes are high. I would be some kind of better off, if only I could decipher this text.

I kneel down in a slanting wind. Every jot and tittle is important. In the pale lamplight of an ice-clad sun, I examine scalloped frills of purple seaweed outlined in pellucid frost. Is this an abbreviation for some other, more familiar word? 'Patience,' perhaps? Or 'courage?' Snow dust fills my footprints from yesterday, which are scribbled amidst a flurry of gull tracks. Even I, a novice at this science, can grasp the gist: 'small part of a big whole,' that's my interpretation of these hieroglyphs.

And what about this crescent sliver of sand? The beach's arms curve open to embrace the waves, which hurry in to enfold the beach, and their joyful exclamations wash my soul as clean as the freshly scoured shore. This ligature – this one character made of two or more letters – I've seen the pattern before. Symbiosis. Give and take. Mutual benefit. I never knew it to be the very essence of this scribe's style.

Walking in, I noticed dead leaves clotting a ditch along the roadside, yet, in the skim of ice covering them I saw living trees reflected from above. How sap rises in spring, in the absence of leaves to generate flow through transpiration and cohesion – this is a mystery not even plant physiologists understand. Maybe the answer is in the seaweed jottings I deciphered just minutes ago: patience and courage.

Just beyond the horizon's razor-straight edge, earth slopes into a curve that would bring me back here once again, were I faithful to the journey. Circles and cycles. The *ductos* of the universe as text unfurls under the hand creating it. As with that ancient style of writing Latin called *boustrophedon*: right to left, left to right, like an ox plowing a field. Or like anyone who notices that another spring will soon be arriving, and we're that much closer to the end of plowing, but some kind of better off. More patient, perhaps, or more courageous? More ready to embrace, with joyful exclamation, that which opens to enfold us?

AFTERWORD

Elizabeth Ayres was not born when John Steinbeck adventured down to Baja California, collecting marine life along the shores and sieving it through writerly sensibilities in *The Log from the Sea of Cortez*. But what boon companions they would have been, this Nobel Laureate from California and this essayist from Maryland's Chesapeake Bay.

"It is advisable to look from the tide pool to the stars and then back to the tide pool again," Steinbeck wrote, and what he meant was that the fullest wonder of the world lies in connecting Nature's minutia with the cosmos, and pondering the miraculous webs of interdependence that entangle humankind. Alone among species we can appreciate the sparkle in a grain of sand alongside the twinkle of galaxies.

This is what Ayres does in terse, rich, poetical language – celebrates cardinals and clouds, decaying tobacco barns and vacant fields along with the physics of the universe, the meaning of light. Solid scientific research and careful observation throughout the book underpin writing that is so lyrical I was lulled into thinking it was all conceived in a glorious fit of inspiration.

"I swam before I walked," Ayres writes; and why not, growing up along the edges of North America's greatest estuary, the Chesapeake Bay, whose land margins fantastically intertwine with tidewater for an estimated 8,000 miles. These seams where ecosystems overlap, whether land-water, forest-field, or the margins of ice fields and drop-offs of continental ocean shelves, are known to scientists, hunters, birdwatchers and beachwalkers alike as the most interesting, lively places in Nature.

Indeed, the progression of the seasons that are structure and inspiration for Ayres' essays are edges, the junctions and intersections and transitions of cold and warmth, the ebb and flow of daylength, the comings and goings of migratory fishes and birds. I once lived three years on a high plateau in eastern Africa said to have the world's most perfect year-round weather. For one used to mid-Atlantic seasons this soon became boring.

Ayres finds nothing boring. Here she is, holding her breath for well over a minute underwater, watching barnacles on an obscure pole stuck down in shallow water: "...pointy little beaks inside each hexagonal shell open... a delicate hand would emerge... spread feathery fingers, wave back and forth. Breaking the spell, I would raise one of my own fingers and bring it up close, quicker than quick, all the tiny doors on all the tiny houses would close up tight... a magic show meant for me alone."

Here she is, walking in the 'swash zone' – that narrow band where surf laps on the shore, pauses and retreats, an edge within an edge – making of it a lovely metaphor for the summer solstice she celebrates that day. Solstice literally means 'sun stop.' This peaking of light's annual wave is yet another edge, a pause before day length begins to shorten, headed from June 21st to the longest darkness of December 21st.

Then there's time she spent living in New York City, New Mexico and beside the Chesapeake, seen intriguingly through the lens of "three moons"... but of course, you have already read it yourself, along with the other celebrations of the mundane and the universal that fill these pages. The unexamined life, it's been said, is not a life worth living. Neither is the unexamined place nearly so worth living in. The beauty and wonder Ayres finds all across her pocket of the planet does proud the Chesapeake region, investing it with value that transcends region.

—Tom Horton, author of *Bay Reflections*,
winner of the 1988 John Burroughs Medal
for a distinguished work of natural history

Veriditas Books

At Veriditas Books, our mission is to publish books and spoken word recordings that foster intimate communion with the natural world, because it is there that humans most readily experience themselves as part of a seamless, vital whole. We believe that the role of the human being is to know, love and serve the aliveness of the universe.

Veriditas Books is a small press dedicated to a large task: assuaging the urgent need for quality literature that connects readers with nature's beauty, wisdom and mystery. We expect to publish two new book titles and two new recordings yearly.

Every living thing has its place of belonging, and in this place, becomes beautiful. Veriditas Books proudly hails from St. Mary's County, Maryland, a peninsula that juts into the Chesapeake Bay like a long narrow pier. We hope our publications help you discover and celebrate your own place of belonging. Please contact us with your questions or concerns:

Veriditas Books
P. O. Box 968
California, MD 20619
1-800-510-1049
VeriditasBooks.com
info@veriditasbooks.com

also from Veriditas Books

the five-part *Invitation to Wonder* audio series

"Elizabeth Ayres is Claude Monet with words."
—Paula Cohen, author of *Gramercy Park*,
a Literary Guild/Book of the Month Club selection

The *Invitation to Wonder* audio series consists of five spoken-word recordings. Each features the melodious voice of Elizabeth Ayres, which carries you away to a place where time stands still and even the most ordinary encounters shimmer with extraordinary promise. Titles in the series are:

Audio One - A Journey through the Seasons. Discover fresh meaning and purpose for your own life's passages in nature's reassuring rhythms.

Audio Two - Celebrating the Journey. Transform your yearly round of ho-hum holidays into the joyous occasions they're meant to be.

Audio Three - A Journey into the Cosmos. Develop a richer understanding of the new cosmology and your place in the universe story.

Audio Four - A Journey into Chesapeake Country. Be transported to Maryland's tidewater region – and the hidden places in your own heart.

Audio Five - A Journey into Divine Presence. Experience a deeper intimacy with that ineffable mystery at the heart of creation.

Whichever spoken-word adventure appeals to you, you will receive...

- **12 reflections from the acclaimed book, Invitation to Wonder;**
- **65 minutes of pleasurable listening;**
- **Your choice of an Mp3 download or a compact disk;**
- **A FREE *Companion on the Journey* Listening Guide;**
- **A joyous, life-affirming experience you will treasure – for yourself, or as a gift.**

More benefits on the next page...

to enhance your *Invitation to Wonder* audio experience, Elizabeth Ayres has created the

Companion on the Journey Listening Guide

Each of the five audios in the *Invitation to Wonder* series has its own *Companion on the Journey* Listening Guide, which will custom-fit the recordings to *your* life. In every 10-page Guide you get:

- Questions to sharpen your awareness of nature's aliveness;
- Advice for deepening your appreciation of the place where *you* live;
- Hints to help you apply nature's wisdom to your own life journey;
- Suggestions for outdoor activities you can share with family and friends;
- An interview with the author;
- 10 color photographs taken by Elizabeth Ayres, so that the beauty which inspired her will inspire you.

Your *Companion on the Journey* Listening Guide comes as a pdf download. It's FREE with your purchase of any spoken word recording.

Great for book clubs or discussion groups!

Learn about each audio in this five-part series on the next pages...

audio one of the five-part
Invitation to Wonder series

A Journey through the Seasons

"These exquisitely written reflections create space for all that is beautiful and true."

—Annie Dillard, Pulitzer Prize-winning author of *Pilgrim at Tinker Creek*

Product Description

The recurring sights and sounds that punctuate our days form a great wheel: spring, summer, autumn, winter, spring, summer, round and round. A selection of some of the book's most popular reflections, this recording carries you from flowering through fruitfulness, from harvest through snowy silence. Listening, you will discover fresh meaning and purpose for your own life's passages in nature's reassuring rhythms. Uplifting and inspiring, this is one trip you won't want to miss.

Product Specifications

MP3 Download: 65 minutes; 12 tracks; $19.95

Compact Disk: 65 minutes; 12 tracks; ISBN-13: 978-0-9845178-3-1; $24.95 (Plus shipping. Maryland residents add 6% sales tax.)

Product Contents

"Song Flows Forth;" "Equinox;" "Reconciling with April;" "Praising Green;" "The Zone;" "Berries, Blossoms, Bunting;" "A Slow and Gentle Easing;" "Joe's Garden;" "Thanksgiving Hallelujah;" "Making Friends with Winter;" "Cardinals;" "Deciphering the Season"

Product Guide

Your audio comes with a downloadable, 10-page ***Companion on the Journey*** **Listening Guide** which will help you sharpen your awareness of nature's aliveness; deepen your appreciation for the place *you* inhabit; understand how nature's wisdom applies to your life journey. It gives you suggestions for outdoor activities you can share, plus 10 color photographs taken by Elizabeth Ayres, so the beauty that inspired her will inspire you.

Turn the page to read about Audio Two of this exciting spoken-word series...

audio two of the five-part
***Invitation to Wonder* series**

Celebrating the Journey

"Elizabeth Ayres sees through a special lens. It reveals to her what others overlook."

-- Rick Boyd, editor, *The Enterprise*

Product Description

The festivals that recur each year are meant to enliven and inspire us, but sometimes – be honest! – they become chores. Transform your ho-hum holidays into heartfelt celebrations by tuning in to this life-affirming recording. You will be guided from New Year's through July Fourth into Columbus Day; from Valentine's Day to Halloween; from Easter and Passover through Christmas, Hanukkah and Kwanzaa. Travel one year with Elizabeth Ayres to reclaim all your years for wonder and joy.

Product Specifications

MP3 Download: 70 minutes; 13 tracks; $19.95

Compact Disk: 70 minutes; 13 tracks; ISBN-13: 978-0-9845178-2-4; $24.95 (Plus shipping. Maryland residents add 6% sales tax.)

Product Contents

"The Journey" (New Year's Day); "Notes of a Native Daughter" (Martin Luther King Day); "Shadows" (Groundhog Day); "Everything Curves" (Valentine's Day); "Passing By" (Easter/Passover); "Maytime Musings" (Mother's Day); "Remembering the Future" (Memorial Day); "Butterfly Q & A" (Independence Day); "The Work We Do" (Labor Day); "Vigil" (Columbus Day); "Baking for the Holidays" (Halloween); "Reverie" (Thanksgiving Day); "Catching the Light" (Christmas/Hanukkah/Kwanzaa)

Product Guide

Your audio comes with a downloadable, 10-page ***Companion on the Journey*** **Listening Guide** which will help you sharpen your awareness of nature's aliveness; deepen your appreciation for the place *you* inhabit; understand how nature's wisdom applies to your life journey. It gives you suggestions for outdoor activities you can share, plus 10 color photographs taken by Elizabeth Ayres, so the beauty that inspired her will inspire you.

Visit InvitationToWonder.com to purchase this recording – or the set of five!

Turn the page to read about Audio Three of this exciting spoken-word series...

audio three of the five-part
***Invitation to Wonder* series**

A Journey into the Cosmos

"Lovely. Shows amazing breadth of thought."

—THOMAS BERRY, AUTHOR OF *THE GREAT WORK* AND *THE UNIVERSE STORY* (WITH BRIAN SWIMME)

Product Description

If you believe we are the universe becoming conscious of itself; if you cherish the interdependence of life on earth in all its manifestations; if you believe our journey began 13.7 billion years ago in a glorious throb of energy and light, then this is your "must have" audio. Discover new images in science for reflection. Encounter new metaphors in nature for understanding. Deepen your appreciation for a story of cosmogenesis that is writing itself into your heart even now.

Product Specifications

MP3 Download: 70 minutes; 13 tracks; $19.95

Compact Disk: 70 minutes; 13 tracks; ISBN-13: 978-0-9845178-1-7; $24.95 (Plus shipping. Maryland residents add 6% sales tax.)

Product Contents

"Seedsong: An Elegy for Thomas Berry;" "What the Light Calls Forth;" "Ghost Ship;" "The Comfort of Green;" "The Pier;" "Knowing the Way by Water;" "Bones;" "Vigil;" "The Barn;" "In Praise of Surf;" "The Field;" "We Shall Be Changed;" "Blue Moon"

Product Guide

Your audio comes with a downloadable, 10-page ***Companion on the Journey* Listening Guide** which will help you sharpen your awareness of nature's aliveness; deepen your appreciation for the place *you* inhabit; understand how nature's wisdom applies to your life journey. It gives you suggestions for outdoor activities you can share, plus 10 color photographs taken by Elizabeth Ayres, so the beauty that inspired her will inspire you.

Visit InvitationToWonder.com to purchase this recording – or the set of five!

Turn the page to read about Audio Four of this exciting spoken-word series...

audio four of the five-part
Invitation to Wonder series

A Journey into Chesapeake Country

"Everybody in Chesapeake Country hears the poetry of wind and water. Many aspire to translate it into human language. Elizabeth Ayres succeeds."

—Sandra Olivetti Martin, *Bay Weekly* publisher and editor

Product Description

Like Thoreau's Walden Pond or Dillard's Tinker Creek, Ayres' Chesapeake Country is both place and metaphor. Exploring this alluring region will bring you face to face with hidden places in your own heart. Herons and gulls, crabs and sea nettles, ghost ships and singing rocks ... even barnacles conspire to reveal to you those secret longings you hardly dare acknowledge, even to yourself. Or heave all that overboard and simply enjoy the ride! Either way, this is a listening experience you will cherish, whether you live near the Bay or far from it.

Product Specifications

MP3 Download: 65 minutes; 12 tracks; $19.95

Compact Disk: 65 minutes, 12 tracks; ISBN-13: 978-0-9845178-0-0; $24.95 (Plus shipping. Maryland residents add 6% sales tax.)

Product Contents

"Bay Betrothal;" "Barnacles and Tides;" "Sea Nettles;" "Blue Crab Etude;" "The Gift;" "Fossils;" "The Bridge;" "Ghost Ship;" "The Moon of My Belonging;" "Keeper of the Light;" "A Different Kind of Wonderful;" "Rock Chorus"

Product Guide

Your audio comes with a downloadable, 10-page ***Companion on the Journey*** **Listening Guide** which will help you sharpen your awareness of nature's aliveness; deepen your appreciation for the place *you* inhabit; understand how nature's wisdom applies to your life journey. It gives you suggestions for outdoor activities you can share, plus 10 color photographs taken by Elizabeth Ayres, so the beauty that inspired her will inspire you.

Visit InvitationToWonder.com to purchase this recording – or the set of five!

Turn the page to read about Audio Five of this exciting spoken-word series...

audio five of the five-part
Invitation to Wonder series

A Journey into Divine Presence

"Elizabeth Ayres transforms ordinary perceptions into mystic beauty."
—Beatrice Bruteau, author of *The Easter Mysteries*

Product Description

The glory of the natural world slakes our thirst for the living God. A singing bird, a field of flowers, the liquid tattoo of waves on sand – such wondrous moments are a direct pipeline to divine presence. Every numinous track on this hour-long recording will reveal to you a new aspect of nature's beauty, wisdom and mystery. Opening to the holiness that lies at the source of all being, you will find yourself joyfully embracing that which opens to enfold you.

Product Specifications

MP3 Download: 70 minutes; 13 tracks; $19.95

Compact Disk: 70 minutes, 13 tracks; ISBN-13: 978-0-9845178-9-3; $24.95 (Plus shipping. Maryland residents add 6% sales tax.)

Product Contents

"Raindrops in the River;" "Naming a Place Called Spring;" "What the Light Calls Forth;" "Woodswalk;" "The Gathering;" "Mimosa Moment;" "The Barn;" "In Praise of Surf;" "Catching the Light;" "The Journey;" "We Shall Be Changed;" "Rock Chorus;" "Still Night, Twin Moons"

Product Guide

Your audio comes with a downloadable, 10-page ***Companion on the Journey*** **Listening Guide** which will help you sharpen your awareness of nature's aliveness; deepen your appreciation for the place *you* inhabit; understand how nature's wisdom applies to your life journey. It gives you suggestions for outdoor activities you can share, plus 10 color photographs taken by Elizabeth Ayres, so the beauty that inspired her will inspire you.

Visit InvitationToWonder.com to purchase this recording – or the set of five!

On the next page ... a special offer if you purchase the entire set...

MP3 downloads

Sold separately, this set would cost $99.75.
Get all five for only $77.00.
That's a savings of $22.95!

Compact Discs

Sold separately, this set would cost $124.75.
Get all five for only $97.00.
(Plus shipping. Maryland residents add 6% sales tax.)
That's a savings of $27.75!

Visit InvitationToWonder.com to place your order.

coming June 2011
from Veriditas Books

Writing the Wave:
Inspired Rides for Aspiring Writers
by Elizabeth Ayres

Catch a wave of creativity . . .

There's a vast ocean of creativity within you – and even if you're doubtful, intimidated, or blocked, you can tap into its power simply by following the exercises in this book.

Designed as small steps, each easy exercise takes only minutes to complete. Yet each step swells the wave in your inner ocean -- you feel a rush of ideas, images and scenes as it crests. The words surge out of your pen and flow freely. It's a joyous writing ride that brings you to new heights of creative accomplishment, no matter what your level of experience.

The surf's up. The water is warm and blue. Are you ready to take the plunge?

"Elizabeth Ayres has thought long and hard about the writing process, and is one of the most seasoned and exemplary practitioners in the field of teaching writing. This book is an invaluable distillation of her insights and experiences. I cannot imagine any beginning or struggling writer not coming away with some inspiration from it."

—PHILLIP LOPATE, EDITOR OF *THE ART OF THE ESSAY* AND *WRITING NEW YORK*

Paperback; 270 pages;
ISBN-13: 978-0-9845178-5-5;
9 x 6 x 0.65 inches; $19.95.

Don't want to "write your wave" alone? An **online course** based on this book is currently accepting registrations. Expand your imagination, build confidence and make writing friendships that will last a lifetime. Visit CreativeWritingCenter.com or call 1-800-510-1049 to find out more.

At your bookstore, online retailers or from Veriditas Books (VeriditasBooks.com).

FREE!
from Veriditas Books

Visit the website
InvitationtoWonder.com.

Sign up to be on our mailing list
and receive a free MP3 download
from the *Invitation to Wonder* audio series

Discover for yourself what G.K. Chesterton meant when he said, "The world will never starve from want of wonders, only from want of wonder."

ABOUT THE AUTHOR

Photo: Larry Tierney

Elizabeth Ayres has been hailed by *New York* magazine, the *Voice of America, New York Newsday*, the *Village Voice* and *The Woodstock Times* for her groundbreaking teaching methods. She's appeared on *The Joey Reynolds Show, The Tom Pope Show,* Bill Thompson's *Eye on Books,* WXRK's *Sunday Magazine,*

WOR's *America in the Morning* and other radio and television shows.

A charismatic workshop leader for over 30 years, Ms. Ayres has taught at New York University and the College of New Rochelle; at the New York Open Center and Ghost Ranch Conference Center; through Poets-in-the-Schools and Poets & Writers; in libraries and other public forums. In 1990 she founded the Elizabeth Ayres Center for Creative Writing (CreativeWritingCenter.com), which offers retreats and online workshops to a global community of aspiring writers.

Elizabeth Ayres holds a Master's degree in Creative Writing from Syracuse University, where she was a Cornelia Ward Fellow. She is the author of *Writing the Wave, Know the Way,* and two Sounds True audio albums. She writes frequently for Maryland newspapers, hosted WRYR's *Soundings* program for three years, and her newspaper column, *Soundings*, received a 'First Place, Feature Column' award from the MDDC Press Association in 2008. She lives with two feline companions in Southern Maryland, where the Potomac and Patuxent rivers meet the Chesapeake Bay.

You're invited to contact Elizabeth by email at Elizabeth@InvitationToWonder.com. Or follow her at: Twitter.com/elizabethayres3. Or visit her website, InvitationToWonder.com.

Breinigsville, PA USA
30 March 2011
258767BV00001B/2/P